POWS AT CAMP JERICHO FREED IN BLACK OPS RAID

AT MORNING'S LIGHT

BY E.P. MOORE

If you like *At Morning's Light,* make sure to read
Out of Da Nang, the first E.P. Moore book!

POWS AT CAMP JERICHO FREED IN BLACK OPS RAID

AT MORNING'S LIGHT

BY **E.P. MOORE**

An E.P. Moore Publishing Book
Published by E.P. Moore Publishing
95 Via Cartaya
SAN CLEMENTE, CA 92673
United States

Copyright 2015 by E.P. Moore
Book design by Dori Beeler
Cover design by Dori Beeler
Editing provided by Sandra Rea
Additional services provided by Full Circle Media & Author Promotions

For information regarding special discounts for bulk purchases, please contact E.P. Moore at 949-680-7795.

ISBN: 978-0-692-26497-3

Every effort has been made to make this book as complete and as accurate as possible. However, there may be mistakes, both typographical and in content.

The purpose of this book is to educate and entertain. The stories are based on real-life events, though names have been for the most part changed to protect identities and privacy. The author and publisher shall have neither liability nor responsibility to any person or entity with respect to any loss or damage caused, or alleged to have been caused, directly or indirectly, by the information contained in this book.

If you do not wish to be bound by the above, you may return this book to the publisher for a full refund.

ACKNOWLEDGMENTS

Though this novel is fictional, the story is based on what I believe to be true accounts. In my lifetime, as a pilot for a major airline, I met a soldier who told me he was a member of a special unit organized after March 29, 1973. He looked up at me from where he sat in a wheelchair while waiting to board my aircraft going to Los Angeles, California and began to chat with me.

After the usual pleasant conversation between strangers, the man told me he had been wounded on a Special Ops Raid organized to bring home detainees that North Vietnam refused to acknowledge they had been holding in their prison camps. That bit of information immediately grabbed my interest. It was then that I realized what a large price this man had paid so others might be free.

It was hard not to become completely consumed by his story as we both waited for my plane to arrive. I listened silently as this man told me about the mission. He said that "A Black Operations Unit" was trained, entered North Vietnam and brought home prisoners that the North Vietnam Government had no plans of releasing.

These prisoners fell into several categories. These men had knowledge of sensitive material; they were pilots and weapons systems operators

that our counterpart in Russia wanted held so they could learn about our Advanced Weapons Systems.

This soldier told me the raid (his mission) took place well after hostilities had ended. A hero and gallant man that was a member of this special operations unit would spend the rest of his life in a wheelchair after participating in this daring raid. He willingly fought for his brothers, his country and its freedoms.

The men and women who have served (and those who serve today) our nation inspire me. To each and every one of them I give thanks. I give thanks to all branches of our Armed Forces. Whether these brave individuals of former wars volunteered or were called to duty, what they have given to our nation can never be repaid. The same holds true for the men and women who don a military uniform today.

Though not a highly publicized statistic, at this time there are still about 2,200 servicemen considered missing in action (MIA). There are 55 incidents of American Servicemen last seen alive but unaccounted for.

To all of those who join the military to serve our country and to all who have come before you, I say thank you for your countless struggles, the sacrifices of your families and the efforts you have made in making our country free. Our nation and its people thank you!

GOD BLESS YOU ALL...

TABLE OF CONTENTS

CHAPTER 1

OPERATION AT MORNING'S LIGHT

It was a warm day in July 1977. As usual, I could be found at my desk having a cup of coffee and reading the morning paper. Robert, my gardener, had arrived and was busily mowing the lawn out front. It was a time in my life where labor-intensive work became more and more demanding for me, so I had hired a handyman to come every Friday at the same time to do the chores that required physical labor. Robert always arrived like clockwork.

A gentle breeze blew through the open window, carrying with it the aroma of freshly cut grass into my office as I waited for my grandson, Kirk. He had been questioning me for months concerning his father's death in a war that had ended several years ago. The boy wanted to know why his father's mission was so secretive. It was always the same questions. Why, when, where? Questions I couldn't answer... until that day in 1977.

Sitting in my office, waiting for the arrival of my grandson, I found myself reminiscing about my time in service to the Corps. I still have a clear memory of the day the IJN (Imperial Japanese Navy) attacked our naval forces in Hawaii. The voice on the radio repeated over and over again that Japanese aircraft launched from carriers came out of

the northwest skies and were attacking Pearl Harbor and our support facilities throughout the Hawaiian Islands. Our country's attackers knew about the importance of an organized attack. Their goal was the destruction of our Navy's fighting fleet. If they could accomplish that mission the Japanese would have the freedom to capture and control all the far-eastern countries and their natural resources without the interference of any allied forces.

As for me, I enlisted in the Marine Corps shortly after the attack on Pearl Harbor… December 7, 1941. My initial training at Parris Island was something I've tried my best to forget. After completing Basic and Advanced Infantry Training my orders came through assigning me to the 1st Marine Division. I had my first taste of battle at Guadalcanal as a Marine PFC in the 1st Battalion, Company C, Platoon 355. What a way to start my career.

To this day I have flashbacks of fighting on one of the Solomon Islands; Guadalcanal. The nightmares never leave me. The hand-to-hand fighting during the night was more ruthless and deadly than in daylight hours. I surmise that more Marines died mercilessly in the night than ever by day. I know because members of my platoon and I found fellow Marines dead in their trenches or foxholes every morning. Memories such as these are difficult to move beyond. They stick with you like gum to your shoe. You carry them with you wherever you go.

Just after dark the Nips as we called them would move quietly from their holes and silently slide into our trenches. It was difficult to tell who might be moving toward you in the darkness. I remember the fear that crept through my veins every night… a fear of killing one of

your own. It was talked about among our men that by the time you recognized the enemy it was too late to protect yourself.

This is how my grandson's father... my son... died; I can only imagine what it was like for him and what ran through his mind at the very end. It may have been a different war, but the fears remain the same. Death at the hands of the enemy has the same horrific outcome. Families are broken all the same.

I keep several of the citations I've earned in battle on the walls of my office. There's a reason. I read and re-read them. They give me strength. After perusing them I find myself visualizing the terrifying and tragic memories of battles that I continue to fight in the theatre of my mind. My hands still tremble as I recall the blackness of night inseparably entangled with the moans of the men who lay wounded and dying. To this day I hear their cries for help and remember how I had to force myself to remain steadfast in my duties. I could not go to the dying man for good reason. Was it an imposter calling us out to meet our death or was it truly a Marine in distress? Too many Marines lost their lives finding out.

Yes, I can still hear their cries. Over, over and over I hear them begging for help. Throughout the night their screams would go on for what seemed like hours before growing weaker and weaker until they were heard no more.

Over the years I've asked myself why I offered no help. To this day I've convinced myself that it was the enemy calling out not a fellow Marine.

CHAPTER 2

THE STORY BEGINS/INSTRUCTOR BILLET

My grandson Kirk was 17 years old and due to arrive at my doorstep at any moment. His mother and I had decided that today was the day to appease his relentless requests about his father's death. It was going to be hard for me to tell the story since it was the tale of my son's death, too. Kirk had the right to know what had happened to his father. He would no longer accept our well-practiced story about his dad being just another causality of the war.

Kirk had been urging his mother, grandmother and me to provide the details of where, when and why his father had been killed in 1975 fighting in a war that had officially concluded in 1972. Why was he awarded medals for bravery without the written citations and with a modest ceremony; just medals delivered to our home in a small box with a single paragraph telling us that the government was sorry for our loss. It wasn't right not knowing the details of his death. Kirk had a right to know the reasons.

A few months earlier our government had declassified and released the names of the units involved along with the personnel who operated under the secrecy of Operation At Morning's Light. Until that happened, I wasn't able to talk about the details of the mission in which Kirk's father was a participant.

Drawing a deep breath, I told myself I would have the strength to tell my grandson the truth. It was time.

I knew that soon Kirk would arrive and I'd be looking at him through the door of my office. Seeing the boy always affected me. Kirk was the spitting image of his dad and every time I looked at him it brought tears to my eyes. An honor student at Del Wilson High School in Santa Rosa County, Florida, he carried himself well as a young adult. His friends were numerous and he never seemed to get into any kind of trouble like so many of his classmates. Kirk avoided smoking, drugs, alcohol and the consequences that went along with those choices. I always told him that his father would be proud of all that he had accomplished these past few years.

Like his father, Kirk stood just short of six feet tall, had golden blonde hair, weighed around 220 pounds, was very muscular from lifting weights constantly and never had any trouble with the ladies. Let's just say his dance card was always full!

Kirk played both middle linebacker on the school's football team and catcher on the baseball team. He was an excellent athlete. The Philadelphia Phillies had been recruiting him since the beginning of his junior season. His mother Martha and I never missed any of his games. It was very cold at a few of those football games, but we stayed strong, shivering in our seats, nearly freezing as we watched him play. Wrapped in wool blankets, we sat on those harsh metal bleachers and refused to go home until we had seen the very last play. Hot chocolate saved us every time. Thank God for the concession stand!

My memories of those frigid days came to an abrupt end as I heard Kirk call out from the front of the house.

"Grandpa, where you hiding?"

I returned his call with a loud, "I'm in the office; come on in."

Seconds later I was looking into the young man's face as he took a seat in the comfortable chair that sat at the front of my desk. The black leather squealed as he shifted back to get comfortable.

After some small talk I brought up the story Kirk so desperately wanted to hear. "Your father had been in the Marine Corps for a total of nine years, completing one tour of duty in Vietnam. With the government's decision to withdraw from combat operations, your father received orders from Headquarters Marine Corps transferring him to the Marine Corps Air Facility Santa Ana, California, for two years and then to Training Squadron One, U. S. Naval Auxiliary Air Station, Saufley Field, Pensacola, Florida."

Kirk looked at me as if I was speaking a foreign language. I knew I'd have to explain a bit more.

"Saufley Field is where all incoming cadets and officers that have the desire and dreams of becoming a pilot begin their initial flight training in the United States Navy or Marine Corps. Your father was to be a flight instructor at his new duty station OLF (Outlying Field) NAS Saufley."

Kirk shifted in his chair again and nodded, so I would know to continue.

"The history of Saufley Field began in 1939 when the Department of the Navy purchased 900 acres northwest of Pensacola, Florida. Construction on an airfield began in early 1939 and was completed by late 1940. The airfield was named after Lieutenant Junior Grade Richard C. Saufley, Naval Aviator #14 who was killed in a training exercise on June 9, 1916.

"The acreage for the field was purchased from an elderly couple in their 80s with a provision in the purchase contract that embraced the couples right to live out the remainder of their lives in their farmhouse on what was soon to be military property. The Department of the Navy agreed. The gentleman passed away in 1943 and his wife in 1948. Their farmhouse of 52 years was torn down sometime in late 1949."

As I watched my grandson's face, I could tell that he wasn't all that interested in the history lesson, but I figured he needed to know it all… every bit of what lead to his father's death. The history of where his father had been trained was important. Maybe one day Kirk would pass the story on to his own sons.

I continued with my story. "Knowing the history of Saufley, attending flight school and completing basic training as a student himself, your dad had first-hand knowledge of the responsibilities that would be required of him and that would one day make him an excellent instructor. If his students had any dreams and aspirations of being successful in the flight training program they would have to

demonstrate to him that they had the ability to master the many tasks and skills in their initial training flights. They had to possess what it would take to continue forward in the program. A significant number of students wash out for one reason or another and only one out of two made it through the program in its entirety to receive their Wings of Gold."

Kirk was now pushing forward in his seat. I had captured his attention.

"Your father's students, whether officers or cadets, had to successfully complete a syllabus of 13 pre-solo and 10 precision acrobatic flights. Every student would have a check ride from a different instructor other than his own on his PS12 and if it was satisfactory PS13 was a solo. No favoritism was shown to Student Officers vs. NavCads or MarCads as all flight training was identical in nature. The only variance for either officer or cadet happened to be ground school. They did not attend classes or courses together as rank structure kept them separated.

"Your father as a MarCad would repeatedly say, I'm lost somewhere between 2nd Lt. USMC / Ensign USN and the highest-ranking enlisted men of both services and no one cares or gives a damn about what I have to say. He was correct. Knowing little of the flight program as an instructor, your dad began his research on what to expect as he transitioned from a fleet pilot in the Marine Corps to instructor at a naval air station in the training command."

Here I stopped to ask if Kirk was following. Again he nodded, giving

me the go-ahead to continue. It felt like he was taking mental notes. Maybe he would become a Marine.

"The aircraft your father would be training all his apprentice airmen in would be the T34B. Built by Beechcraft Corporation the T34B Mentor was a two place, tandem, low-wing, single-engine trainer. To meet the requirements as an instructor in that aircraft your dad had to master and complete the identical syllabus as a student only he had to be considerably more proficient in the required maneuvers."

"Your dad had six weeks of comprehensive classroom study on aircraft systems and procedures in the T34B given to him by a special tutorial instructor. After successfully passing and completing ground school he was then required to satisfactorily complete the identical syllabus a student would receive. At that point he was transferred to Flight 18 at Saufley Field to instruct primary flight students. He was to proceed with caution in molding Marine Corps and Naval Juvenile Fledglings."

I was throwing a lot of information at my grandson, but he seemed to be keeping up. I wanted him to know how hard his father had trained and how good an instructor he was.

I shifted forward in my seat so I could make better eye contact with Kirk before continuing. "The pilot training center at Saufley was an enormous hanger positioned at the south end of the field. It was divided into four sections, one of which was flight 18 the Marine section. The other three sections were strictly for the Naval Students and Naval Instructors. That was segregation at its finest!

"Flight 18's section had four areas: one filled with card tables to use while instructors debriefed students, another area filled with lockers for uniforms and flight gear, a small ready room filled with chairs that had the flight board, hanging on its wall. Off to the right was a Do Not Enter area! This area was for instructors only and if a student came into it uninvited he was doomed... destined for disaster.

Located on the wall at the left as you entered Flight 18's section was a large chalkboard with blocks of names in columns. The instructors' names were written in black; written below those names were the names of each instructor's students. Names were written in green for Marine and blue for Naval students getting their check ride from a Marine instructor.

Beside each student's name in brown was the identifying flight number of his up-and-coming training flight. Atop the student's name was an area all the instructors called THE BOX. It was a small area for the instructor to chalk in either an arrow pointing up or down. Up was okay; down meant paperwork had to be filled out with the instructor's recommendation for either dropping the student from the program or giving two extra flights and a re-check. THE BOX was a visual reminder to me that a student could get a down."

"Wow," said Kirk. "That's tough."

"Yes, it's grueling. Looking for Flight 18's Duty Officer, your dad told me he was stunned to see written on the flight board two Marines he personally knew from his squadron HMM 374 the Red Foxes. Two of his squadron buddies and very close friends that he had flown considerable combat sorties with while stationed at Da Nang Airbase

in Vietnam. He couldn't believe his eyes. On one of those missions, his wingman Lt. William Allen and his co-pilot Lt. Chris Hughes had saved his life after he had been shot down during a medical evacuation sortie following the NVA Siege of Khe Sanh."

"Your father told me that seeing both names on the Flight Board as flight instructors brought back memories of the only time the enemy ever shot him down in Vietnam. Losing control of his aircraft after being hit in the tail rotor, his aircraft had spun, swirled and twisted as it fell from the sky uncontrollably and through some trees before crashing into a shallow riverbed."

"Grandpa, was he hurt?" Kirk's eyes were as big as saucers. He was into the story now. No doubt about it. His dad was a hero and he knew it.

I shook my head. "By the Grace of God, the crew suffered only minor injuries from the impact of crashing. His Crew Chief had a broken arm and your dad's leg had been punctured by one of the branches of a tree. Even with their injuries the entire crew had the presence of mind to have their weapons drawn so they could fire at the pursuing NVA. Your dad told me that the noise was deafening as they fired their weapons, keeping the enemy at bay, while Lt. Allen landed his aircraft at the crash site to pick them up. Your dad said, 'That's the first time in my life that I've had an adrenalin rush.' It came from his fear of being captured by the enemy. When you're really frightened what used to take you five minutes to do you can do in seconds."

"Luckily all of the men safely scrambled aboard Lt. Allen's aircraft. While Lt. Allen was climbing the helo up and out of danger, your

dad told me he remembered frightening sounds he'd never forget. It was coming from round after round of enemy ground fire repeatedly striking the aircraft. Returning fire from the Crew Chief and Side Gunner made little difference to suppress the enemy fire. Then suddenly Lt. Allen yelled out in pain, 'I'm hit in the calf... a through and through!'"

"Oh, my God, Grandpa," exclaimed Kirk. "What then? What next?"

"Well, Lt. Allen passed the word over the intercom to his crew chief to tell your dad during the climb out, 'You owe me one, Ryan, and if I ever go down you better come get my ass!' Your dad screamed over the noise of the engine to the crew chief and said, 'Tell him I give my word; I'll be there for him and I owe him a beer.'"

At this point in the story, my grandson was beaming. His old man was one cool dude. That's what the expression on his face told me.

I smiled at Kirk and kept going. "On the way home Benson, the Crew chief, passed the emergency medical kit to the Lt. so he could place a tourniquet over his wound to stop the bleeding. Co-pilot Lt. Hughes took over at the controls and flew the aircraft. All in all, everything worked out for the best. Lt. Allen, or Willie as the men called him, received the Purple Heart and six weeks rest and relaxation... also known as R and R... on the island of Okinawa, Japan. That injury authorized him a comfortable BOQ room at the Marine Air Base Futenma, numerous Hotsi Baths in Naha and who knows what else at the Grand Hotel!" I chuckled, not sure if my grandson knew what I meant or not.

"The Hospital Corps or Mash Unit grounded your father, disallowing all flight duty for two weeks so Colonel Karman, his Commanding Officer, gave him duty that was less fascinating than Lt. Allen's assignments. Your dad was transferred from his normal duties in the Maintenance Department to Operations Officer in S3, which made him responsible for assigning pilots to various missions or Frag Orders that came from the Chain of Command or Headquarters."

"Your dad called it 'the Death Board,' because he hated consigning names on the mission board. He told me that he had a certain amount of guilt if anyone were to be killed or wounded. To place someone's name on that board was exceptionally painful for him because he never knew what the day would bring."

"Getting back on track and concentrating on the scheduling of Flight 18's students and instructors assignments, your dad could see that Willie was out on a flight giving a check ride to one of the Naval Cadets from Flight 19. All he could do was await his return. Continuing to read the flight board he saw Lt. Hughes had already checked in at the OD desk and put an up arrow in THE BOX of his student.

"That meant Hughes had to be somewhere in the instructor's ready room making entries in his student's official flight jacket. All the maneuvers performed that day by a student had to be recorded as above average, average, below average or unsatisfactory and it was the duty of the instructor to record the grades immediately. That way there were no mistakes in grading the maneuver or guesstimating the grade at a later date.

"Low and behold, there was Hughes standing at his locker changing into his uniform when they both spotted each other. It was a monumental and unexpected surprise to see one another after parting ways in Vietnam several years earlier. Your dad told me that Chris yelled across the room to him, 'Well, if it isn't the guy who owes me free drinks for the rest of my life. What in the world are you doing here in Pensacola?"

Here I took a bit of a dramatic pause to see if Kirk was following my story. So far so good. I winked at him before continuing.

"Responding with a crack in his voice, your dad said, 'I really wanted A4's but Marine Corps Headquarters thought otherwise and here I am like you, grinding out future Naval Aviators. Most will be flying helos pretty soon. The rumor has it five out of ten Cadets are going into choppers or multi-engines out of the Command."

Kirk listened intently as his grandpa continued with the story of his father's military life.

"Lt. Allen, Lt. Hughes and your dad would be inseparable friends for the rest of their lives, Kirk. Your dad used to say, 'I owed them everything, but all they've ever wanted in return was a thank you, a Semper Fi and a few strong drinks from the O Club!'"

Just then, Kirk's Grandma walked in and asked, "What's going on?" After catching her up she agreed it was time to tell Kirk all he wanted to know. She nodded to us as if giving us her permission to proceed. "Do you fellows want anything to eat or drink?"

Responding in one voice we both said, "No, but thanks anyway." We were trying to be polite, but Kirk was sitting in my office for a reason and I was anxious to get back to the story.

"Let's see… where were we?" I quipped. "Oh! Your dad was in the ready room with Lt. Hughes, about to make his way to the OD and check in. Okay, I'll take it from there."

Kirk smiled as if to say, "Yeah, let's go!"

"Giving Chris a firm handshake and a goodbye your dad turned to make his way back to the OD desk for his check in and yelled to his old friend, 'Promise me you'll contact Willie so the three of us can rendezvous at the O Club Mainside at 1800 hours. Yesterday was payday so I've got a lot of cash on hand for French 75s and I owe you both a good drunk.'

"Giving his attention to the Duty Officer your dad introduced himself. Without hesitation the Duty Officer placed his name on the board and assigned your dad four students that had been waiting a week for their instructor. One junior brown bar, or 2nd Lt. USMC and three Marine Cadets would be his first students."

All four stood before him with pride in their hearts and eyes full of apprehension. Their concerns were real as they looked for reassurance from your dad. Like any Cadet or Student Officer, I'm sure that they all hoped and prayed that Captain Ryan was a mild-tempered individual and not a screamer. The latter didn't make for great trainers."

Looking Kirk straight in the eyes, I told him that the information I was giving him were things the boy's father had told him over the phone or in letters he had written to your grandmother and me.

I could tell that Kirk was happy to know what happened early on, but wanted me to get to the heart of the story. I wasn't going to be rushed, because I wanted him to know what kind of person his dad was to the men around him and also to know how he dealt with his role as an instructor.

"As I said before, your dad had checked in at Ops and was immediately given four new students. He told me that he called them one by one to a training table in the corner of the ready room. He introduced himself and told them a little about who he was, so they could feel more comfortable with their training. He told them each that he was a farm boy from Wyoming, Delaware, who enlisted in the Corps after completing two years of college. "Like you" he said, "I was a Marine Cadet. I've walked in your shoes, so I know what it's like to be where you are now."

"Wow," said Kirk. It seemed like the boy hadn't heard anything about his dad before, or maybe it just took on a new meaning now that he was coming of age.

"Yep, that's right," I said. "It took almost two years of concentrated study and effort before he received his Wings of Gold. That was back in July of 1967. Receiving orders from Headquarters Washington, he was then transferred to a helicopter squadron, HMM 374, at the Marine Corps Air Station Tustin… Tustin, California."

I looked at Kirk to see if he had any questions, but the boy was silent and all ears as he kept leaning forward in his seat.

"After six months of intensive and rigorous training in the Santa Ana Mountains and on carriers off the coast of Pendleton, your dad's squadron went directly to Da Nang, Vietnam. That was in late January of 1968. His only stop was in Anchorage, Alaska, to refuel the aircraft and replenish their food supplies. How about that?"

I told Kirk that his dad was really good at giving other people credit. When he told his Cadets about his experience, he would tell them, "In the FMF (Fleet Marine Force) I flew the UH34D, a helicopter built by Sikorsky. In combat I received the DFC (Distinguished Flying Cross) for a mission I flew in Vietnam. Please do not look at me as if I am a hero. It was just by chance that I was at the right place at the wrong time. The real heroes are instructors like Captain Chris Hughes and Captain William Allen. I owe them my life. I went down and they saved my ass."

My son told the Cadets these things because he wanted them to approach their duties with honor and integrity, too.

He told them, "You have to and are expected to know on every flight all your procedures from gear up to gear down and everything in between. Know all your procedures cold. Knowing the maneuvers and applying them in flight is essential to your success. If you don't know your procedures you're predestined to failure or misfortune."

He continued as each Cadet listened intently. "I want you to know that I will give you some slack; I have a soft touch... to a degree. Only because I was a Cadet. While under my training and supervision you are allowed one day of grace or forgiveness. If you do not want to fly or are ill prepared, hung-over, sick and just don't want to go up that day you will be waived that period of instruction and granted one cancellation free of charge. Just tell me you'd rather not fly that day and you can walk away, no questions asked."

After the introductions, both students and instructor felt good about one another and knew what to expect.

Kirk's expression told a story. He was amazed at the man he was learning about and didn't recognize him as his father. "Grandpa, how come he was a Teddy Bear to his students and always so hard on me?"

"That's the way it is sometimes, young man," I said, ruffling the kid's hair. "You'll see one day when you have kids. We're different people in different situations. He was tough on you for a reason maybe. He wanted you to be able to handle yourself, no matter what. Plus, once you've been through a war, you change. He loved you, but you know that, right?"

Kirk nodded in the affirmative.

CHAPTER 3

THE UNEXPECTED HAPPENS

K irk wanted me to get back to the story, so I did.

"It was about one week later when the unexpected happened. The day started as it always would with your dad checking in at muster, glancing at the flight board to see which of his students would be the first to start the day. With the briefing completed both instructor and student made their way to their designated aircraft out on the tarmac or flight line."

"MarCad Adams, who happened to be on his second flight (PS2, pre-solo two), had about one hour and thirty minutes in type (T-34). PS2 had the student making his first take off, climbing to an altitude, leveling off and then entering into slow flight."

I stopped here, because I could see Kirk didn't exactly know what that meant. I told him that, "slow flight is a procedure where the gear and flaps are extended and the aircraft flown at minimum speed while he as the instructor emphasizes and draws attention to the importance of trimming the forces (using the trim tabs) out of the flight controls so the aircraft is easy to fly."

Kirk nodded, so I proceeded.

"So far, Adams had received an above average in performing the preflight of the aircraft, completion and use of the checklists, engine start procedures and radio procedures with ground control and tower. Your dad said Adams was doing okay, or as he always said, 'So far, so good!'

"Your dad told me on that day that the takeoff was just average for a PS2 as Adams had a bit of a problem keeping the nose of the aircraft on the centerline of the runway. The aircraft kept wandering left to right, right to left, throughout the entire takeoff roll. Adams kicked the rudder pedals back and forth, trying to steer the aircraft, which was normal for a student on his first takeoff. The climb-out and level off at 6,500 feet was just average, but then without warning smoke started to enter the forward cockpit!"

Here I added a dramatic pause before telling the rest of the story. "Your dad had to take control of the aircraft from Cadet Adams, declared an emergency or mayday on guard (frequency 121.5 on the radio) and started to look for a field to make a landing while beginning the engine fire checklist. He told me his gut was churning. He needed a place to land and fast. Any farmer's field would do as long as it was long and level. He immediately told Adams over the intercom, 'Open your canopy and prepare to bail out if and when I give the order!' In all the excitement Adams screamed out over the intercom, 'Flames are starting to enter the forward cockpit area!' Your dad wasn't too ruffled. He had already moved the fuel cut-off switch to the off position. However, the engine continued to run, which spelled danger."

Kirk's eyes widened. "Man... what then, Grandpa?"

"Well, your dad screamed over the intercom, "Adams, bail out. I'll follow you out once you're over the side."

Adams just sat there. You're going to have to pardon my French, but your dad told him, 'If you fail to go now you're burnt toast. Get your fucking ass out of the aircraft now. That's an order!' Yet Adams sat frozen in his seat, paralyzed by fear.

I went on to explain what transpired next, telling Kirk that his dad thought he could trick the Cadet into unbuckling his seatbelt.

My son tried to calm the Cadet. He said, "Just unbuckle your seat belt and get on top of the pilot seat in a squat position to keep from getting burned." The Cadet did as he was told. That's where things got really exciting.

"You know what happened next, Kirk?"

"No, Grandpa... what?"

"Once the Cadet had unbuckled his seat belt and moved into a squatting position, your dad rolled the aircraft inverted and within seconds they were both freefalling from about 3,000 feet! Thirty seconds later, as they were safely descending downward in their open chutes, their aircraft Number VT 14 exploded. They were two incredibly lucky Marines having exited the aircraft when they did or they would have been on the Marine Corps monthly accident report as two fatalities!"

Kirk's eyes grew even wider.

"Another aircraft from Flight 18 that happened to be in the area and had heard your dad's mayday call saw them as they were descending into an open field about 20 miles northwest of Saufley. I guess he had reported back to the command that they were both out of the aircraft, chutes open and requested that the search and rescue helicopter be launched for their recovery."

The recovery was quick; within 45 minutes they were in the SAR Helo with a Navy Corpsmen checking them out to see if they had any injuries. They were fine. Their return trip to home base wasn't exactly how they planned it, but they were thankful, safe and without injury.

"Kirk, your dad was something else! Brave man. Smart. He told me that with their feet on Terra Firma back at Saufley without delay Adams and he went directly to the line shack requesting Seaman Graves and McGovern. They were the men who had packed their parachutes and they wanted to thank them for saving their lives. Your dad told me that they wanted to do something to reciprocate.

"One of them responded deadpan in a serious tone, 'Well, Sir, we want one blue and one white brand new BMW Convertible.' Then they all broke out in laughter.

"Your dad said, 'Sorry, but that request is out of the question. What you will receive is a favorable reputation, an outstanding fitness report and a free drunk. Name your time and place. How about Trader Jon's, Saturday night at 1930 hours?'"

Kirk laughed. "I wish I could have been there."

"Me too Kirk, me too. Your dad told me that Adams, Graves, McGovern and he spent the next two weeks giving speeches to all the different commands about the good and the bad about fire in an aircraft. The bad being the fire; the good being their chutes opened. Seaman Graves and McGovern got all the attention. As it should be. A whole lot of pilots owe their lives to packers."

"Cool story, Grandpa," Kirk interrupted. "What about that At Morning's Light mission? You said something about that before."

"I'm getting to it," I said, winking at the boy. "In the meantime Operation At Morning's Light was well into the planning stages by the Joint Chiefs. Little did your father know, but his name was on page 23, listing him as a possible participant. The Office of Naval Intelligence was and had been doing a background check on your dad for a Top Secret Clearance."

CHAPTER 4

THE JOINT CHIEFS
AT MORNING'S LIGHT PERSONNEL

I explained to my eager grandson that the sole purpose of the Joint Chiefs is to plan operations, command readiness and be responsible for the training of their respective services and combatants. Along with their collective responsibilities, they are the primary advisors to the President of the United States, the Secretary of Defense and the Assistant Secretary of Defense.

Using the expertise of the Joint Chiefs of Staff, a special unit of Professional U.S. Marines would be selected, ordered and transferred to a confidential area located within the confines of the Marine Base Camp Pendleton, Oceanside, California.

I explained to Kirk that in regard to his father's mission, a security check on each and every individual had been ongoing for at least six months. This operation had been in the pipeline and studied by the staff members of the Joint Chiefs for quite sometime but little effort had been organized until most recently. It went from a maybe to a Top Secret Operation.

Since the group as a whole would be an all Marine unit the Commandant of the Marine Corps as a member of the Joint Chiefs wanted to personally approve each and every individual. It was noted

in the footnotes on one of the pages that every selectee had been decorated for heroism during the Vietnam War. He wanted the best of the best.

The Commandant selected the team while the Joint Chiefs had the operation planned by staff members stationed throughout the Pentagon. Portions of the operation were already in motion.

General Royal J. Grayson, the Commandant of the Marine Corps would make the final assessment of the individuals he wanted on this team. His staff could either approve or disapprove, but with just a single disapproval by any member on the selection committee that selected individual would be eliminated from the team. After a long and burdensome process the Commandant and the Joint Chiefs forwarded their encrypted Recommendations and Operational Plans to the Secretary of Defense and the President of The United States using the code words "At Morning's Light."

Along with the likelihood and probability of this mission drawing to a successful conclusion, a percentage figure was inserted in the final paragraph. That figure was 95% only after reviewing the selectees of this unit. These men had been chosen because their commitment, faithfulness and heroism under extreme conditions and hardships as demonstrated numerous times in Vietnam. This left little doubt to the selection board that they would and could bring this mission to a successful conclusion with the least amount of disorder, mayhem or chaos. The President signed all the necessary documents with his comment in the lower right hand corner: "With enthusiasm, RWR."

Now that I had made sure Kirk understood the process, so he would also know that not everyone in the service would be chosen for important missions, I continued my story.

"Months passed as your dad continued to carry out his normal duties when unexpectedly the OD approached him with a message from Colonel Raymond. Raymond was his Commanding Officer and the CO of the Marine Detachment at NAS (Naval Air Station) Mainside in Pensacola, Florida. The CO requested your dad's presence in his office immediately.

"Your dad found his students waiting for him in the Ready Room and informed them that their scheduled flights regrettably had to be cancelled. His final words to his students were to study their procedures in his absence, be solidly prepared for their next flight and to wait in Flight 18's Ready Room until his return. If he hadn't returned by 1500 hours they were dismissed for the day."

Kirk was all ears now. He was finally getting to the part he'd been waiting to hear.

"Making his way to the parking lot your dad jumped into his 65 Ford Mustang Convertible," I continued. "He loved that car! He went home, took a quick shower, put on his summer khaki uniform and then made his way to the Marine Detachment at NAS Pensacola. A quick six-mile drive and he was in the Colonel's office, body and soul filled with apprehension. He was so restless that he couldn't stop moving. Your dad couldn't think of any reason he'd be dressed down and criticized. He told me he thought an ass chewing was in the picture, but failed to see any reason whatsoever for being called in to the CO's office. He had fulfilled all his requirements in the training of his students, passed all his tests for promotion and yet here he was being ordered to the CO's office without any reason for him to be taken off the flight schedule and ordered to the Snake Pit."

"In a firm voice the OD of flight 18 had said, 'Just get over to Colonel Raymond's office immediately.'"

"Uh, oh," whispered Kirk.

"Yeah, your dad's concerns were understandable," I said.

"Headquarters Marine Corps had a new set of orders for him. Sealed in a large manila envelope that had been hand-carried by currier and passed along to him by a Marine Captain who had come from the Pentagon with 'Special Orders' and labeled 'Captain Jason E. Ryan 085960 USMC.'"

"Kirk, what I have told you so far came from letters, phone calls and information passed along from your mother and bits that your father was able to share with me months ago. The remainder of this story you so comprehensively want to know came from additional information received from the Marine Corps."

"Your father kept us up to date on his duties, within certain limitations, of course and always stayed within the guidelines of his military orders with the information that he was authorized to provide your mother and me. I'll tell you everything I know."

Kirk shrugged and shot me a half smile.

"As I have already disclosed to you, your dad's story really begins at the office of his Commanding Officer where he received extraordinary and unexpected orders from Headquarters Marine Corps," I added. "He kept a log from the time of his transfer to the date of his death and the material gathered from this log or journal is best told to you as if you were hearing it from your dad. "

AS I REMEMBER IT, IT WENT SOMETHING LIKE THIS...

CHAPTER 5

SEALED ORDERS
CAPTAIN JASON E. RYAN 085960 USMC

Determining from my Military Identification Card that I was indeed the proper person for whom the orders were written the currier's only words to me were, "Sign here on the dotted line." After signing the official document of acceptance he turned to Colonel Raymond my Commanding Officer and asked him to sign beneath my name as a witness to receiving such orders. With that the currier turned away and I watched as he walked down the passageway, opened the double doors and departed the office without saying another word.

Written on the outside of the envelope in bold black print:

ONLY FOR THE EYES OF CAPTAIN JASON E. RYAN 085960 USMC. READ, COMPLY and BURN ALL PAGES EXCEPT PAGE 23a. Open and read page 23a immediately. Have present Commanding Officer of your unit (Vt-1) present and cut orders of transfer as soon as possible.

That particular page instructed me to proceed to Marine Corps Base Camp Pendleton, Oceanside, California. The page read, "You are to report directly to Brigadier General Paul Gardner, Deputy Commander U. S. Marine Corps Forces, Special Operations

Command." It was underlined, <u>Report to and only him no later than November 1, 1973.</u>

After the currier departed Colonel Raymond spoke briefly thanking me for my commitment to duty and dedication to my students. I was surprised to hear that several of them had written a review on me upon completion of their syllabus and passed it via the chain of command to Colonel Raymond to tell him how I had worked to the limit in planning their success.

Colonel Raymond said, "It will be noted in your final Fitness Report from my Command your dedication to your students and position as a flight instructor. At times it is tiresome and thankless and yet you passionately fulfilled your duties. I will immediately start the process for your transfer to Camp Pendleton as directed and they will be ready for pick up by 1600 hours or 1800 hours at the latest. I just want to add this and tell you as I look directly into your eyes... you are a Marine's Marine. I wish I could pin a ribbon on your chest for heart. God Bless. Thank you for your service to God, Country, Corps."

At that point, I turned to leave Command and return to Saufley.

As far as flying another flight with my apprentice students, there was little time left in the day and even less desire on my part. Flying a training flight at the moment was out of the question.

I felt a certain amount of concern knowing my students would be given a replacement instructor within the next couple of days. I was blameless as to what was taking place and confident they would recognize that all military personnel must accept legal orders

or special assignments given to them by their superiors without question, students included.

I knew their individual desires were to receive a replacement instructor that was compatible in spirit, possessed core values akin to mine and not someone new to the command as their instructor.

The student-instructor relationship has a lot to do with a student's success. If it's positive it's beneficial; if it's negative it could be disastrous. My transfer was not planned, requested or applied for. I had my orders and I will carry them out to completion. I could only wish my students well.

Returning to Saufley I saw my students seated at one of the debriefing tables located at the far corner of the room. As I approached I was greeted by a collection of puzzled looks. My students knew that something of significance had materialized at Colonel Raymond's office. They also knew the consequence of whatever it was. It would have an emotional impact on them as well. It's called "collateral damage."

The moment I made eye contact with them, they knew misfortune was around the corner. I knew the look. They assumed they were about to be assigned a new instructor and frustration filled the room as I informed them I was being transferred to Marine Corps Base Camp Pendleton.

The prospect of adjusting to a new instructor was unforeseen to us all. I let them know that they were all doing well in the program and

they shouldn't worry. They would do well with any instructor and then I promised them I would do my best to select someone who used guidelines similar to those that I used in my training. I told them that I would also tell their new instructor about how I committed to each of them one day of grace and how it works. So far, none of them had exercised his day of forgiveness.

The look on their faces told me they feared the worse. Cadet Kale said, "I hope it won't be someone like Captain D. B. Foster, Call Sign Chanel #5." Everyone in the room groaned in support of what Kale had just said.

Captain Foster was due to pick up a brand new series of students and my students, one and all, feared the worse, imagining their names posted on the Flight Board in Operations below his.

Foster was a JERK (in capital letters) and had a history throughout VT-1 as the biggest asshole in the command. He carried a water pistol on all his flights that was filled with perfume in his helmet bag. When his students would error in performing a required maneuver Foster would spray the back of their necks with perfume as punishment.

News travels fast and everyone in Flight 18 took sides with Foster's newest student. Foster directed his student, Lt. Wesley, to taxi the aircraft to the engine run-up area after only being in the cockpit of the T34 less than five minutes. Foster knew his student had no idea where to go, so he used his perfume pistol three times before Wesley had the aircraft underway.

In as respectful a tone as Lt. Wesley could muster, he spoke to Captain Foster on the Ground Control Radio Frequency instead of the aircraft's intercom. That way a copy of what was said would be recorded in the tower and everyone monitoring ground control would hear what was actually said.

Lt. Wesley said calmly, "Captain Foster, please refrain from spraying me with your perfume pistol or there will be serious consequences when PS1 is terminated or completed."

Hearing those words, the enraged Foster took the aircraft from Lt. Wesley, returned to the ramp area. He to Wesley, "You have a down for headwork and another unsatisfactory for insubordination." The whole exchange was heard over ground control as Lt. Wesley keyed his mike as Captain Foster screamed at him while taxing the aircraft back to the blocks.

The crew chief assigned to the aircraft for the day was surprised to see his aircraft VT 23 returning to spot 6 and assumed something mechanically was wrong with the aircraft. It wasn't unusual for crews to go through a rolling checklist while taxiing the aircraft, find something wrong with a system and return to the blocks. This wasted little time and enabled the instructor and student to get another aircraft so he could complete the exercise or task.

Securing the aircraft on spot 6, both student and instructor unstrapped from their seats, got out of the aircraft and hit the ground. Seaman Spain witnessed Lt. Wesley walk up to Captain Foster and nail him with a right to the jaw, laying him out flat on his back for about three minutes.

Struggling to get back on his feet Foster growled, "I promise you...
I will be recommending you for a Court Martial with the charge of
assault and battery on a superior officer."

Within the hour, Seaman Pearlman, the Crew Chief of the T34, handed
Captain Foster and Lt. Wesley a copy of the recording he retrieved
from the tower of their conversation. All naval personnel working
in the area of the flight line who had observed the entire event were
in the office of Flight 18's CO, standing tall in front of the harshest
disciplinarian in the Corps, Major A. E. Goldsborough, USMC.

Soliciting information from all persons either directly or indirectly
involved as observers or participants, they were questioned one by
one and then dismissed. At that point Lt. Wesley received an apology
from Major Goldsborough who assigned him a new instructor and
told him, "Lt. Wesley, you are excused from this hearing and my
office."

At that point only Captain Foster remained in the office, standing at
attention in front of Major Goldsborough. Foster's perfume weapon
was confiscated and he received a severe scolding from Major
Goldsborough. Foster was then relieved of his duties, confined to the
Bachelor Officer's Quarters until further notice and told a possible
Court Martial was in his near future. In the closing stages of his
reprimand, Hard Ass (as all the officers in flight 18 called him) was
speaking so loudly that all those in the immediate area could hear his
last words to Captain Foster. "Get out of my office! I can't stand the
sight of a piece of shit!"

My students recognized the value of Captain Foster's reprimand and accepted my promise that they would receive an instructor that was substantially more to their liking. I was as apologetic as I could be in communicating to them that I would be unable to continue as their mentor throughout the remainder of their primary training schedule. I wished them luck and told them that when our paths crossed again I expected that they would be 2nd Lieutenants in the Marine Corps, wearing their coveted Wings of Gold.

After shaking hands with each of the men, I was proud to receive their customary salute. We parted ways in the hanger area, sharing a great sense of apprehension and anxiety. None of us had a crystal ball; none of us knew what the future held. The only words that escaped our lips as we departed the area in search of our cars were the honored words spoken from one Marine to another, "Semper Fi, Marine, Semper Fi."

CHAPTER 6

MEMORIES OF THE PAST

Arriving home, my next painful endeavor was to tell Martha that I had received special orders requiring my immediate departure to a new assignment. Martha was excited until I told her that she was to remain behind with Kirk and that I was unable to take my family along to wherever it was that I was being sent.

I tried to tell Martha it was especially important for Kirk to remain here as a student at Del Wilson High as he had multiple opportunities available to him through sports and academics and it would be catastrophic if we transferred him to a new school at this point in time. The coaches, teachers and counselors would not be aware of or have knowledge of his background and probably would be ill at ease in helping him to solicit or petition for scholarships or baseball contracts.

Martha began to sob. I couldn't console her. She knew the risks of a special and very secret assignment just as much as I did. This wasn't the first time we had been separated over the years.

As I watched the tears run down Martha's cheeks, all I could do is hold her in my arms. I understood completely, but there wasn't anything I could do to soften her grief. As my wife, she had endured

a lot of loneliness and pain as the Marine Corps sent me everywhere and anywhere to do anything and everything… and then eventually sent me off to the war in Vietnam. I survived that experience and now we would go through yet another separation and I didn't even know how long.

Martha told me that she didn't want to be one of those wives who received those painful letters from the Chaplin. She knew a few such wives who lived on our street that had received one of those frightful letters while I was in Vietnam. Martha recounted a tale of one such wife she had remembered well.

She had looked out the window to see a military vehicle pull up and park in front of our home. A Chaplin along with two officers exited the vehicle and began to make their way up the sidewalk to one of the two doors of our unit that faced the street. Terror overtook Martha's mind. She prayed they weren't coming to our door, feeling guilty for praying it wouldn't be ours.

As the Chaplin and his military escorts approached and knocked on the front door to her left Martha became hysterical not for herself but for Penny, our neighbor and good friend. On that day, luck in its strangest form, had visited Martha. It was Penny's door the visitors were knocking upon. Grief and relief left scars on Martha's heart that day. She constantly worried that one-day the knock would be at her door.

Penny was a stunning woman about 28 years of age, tiny in physique and beautiful to all who passed. Her husband was a 1st Lieutenant and had been in the Corps for about four years. They were college

sweethearts who had fallen in love and married immediately upon graduating from the University of New Mexico.

The Lieutenant's Reserve Officer Training Corps (ROTC) scholarship was not a "free" education. It came with great costs; nothing is free in the military. Opportunity is there, but you must earn your way to success. The ROTC scholarship obligated the man to six years' active duty upon graduation. He had gone through and completed Basic School at Camp Barrett Quantico, Virginia, studying weapons, tactics and leadership.

Following his promotion to 1st Lt. and then designated a qualified Platoon Leader, he was given his first command. Before he could catch his breath he was transferred to Vietnam. He had been in country (slang for being in Vietnam) less than a month when he was killed while on patrol near Hill 881 Northwest of Khe Sanh. Forever his wife would remember the name of Hill 881. 10 clicks or 6.2 miles northwest of Khe Sanh, Vietnam.

The couple had two small children, ages 1 and 3. Martha knew what was running through Penny's mind after receiving the news about her husband's death. What were they to do without a father to teach, guide and plan with them their futures? Why was it her husband that had to be taken from her? He was such a good man who loved and cared for his family! He was an overachiever that came from a humble background, having or living most of his life in nothing more glamorous than a four-room, one-story bungalow.

Penny told Martha all about how her husband had walked to school every day until he had saved enough money doing odd jobs for the

neighbors to purchase a beat-up bicycle on its last legs from one of his classmates. He fixed the flat tires, all the dents and painted it candy apple red. From that point, he rode his bike to and from school and was fortunate enough to buy himself a paper route for one dollar and fifty cents from a kid that was going off to college. Delivering the New Mexico Tribune on his bicycle throughout the neighborhood made him three dollars a week, a fortune at that time for a kid his age.

He knew what it was like to be poor. The phone was always being disconnected and reconnected. The fuel supplier who filled the 60-gallon drums in the basement with oil stopped delivery for the furnace for non-payment. At times it was bitter cold for lack of oil to burn in the stove to keep the house warm. The memories of his past kept reminding him that there had to be something more in life. All he had to do was find the pathway that would lead him to a more productive future.

There were mornings when he went to school with an empty stomach. His memories were still fresh when he met his future wife. He told your mother and I the story of when he was a young boy he would wake up early in the morning, wander down to the chicken coop, sit next to the hen's nest and wait for her to lay an egg so he could have a healthy breakfast before school. He was a wonderful young man who fought hard for his success and was taken from this world too soon.

What seemed like hours yet less than 30 minutes the Chaplin and his staff departed, leaving Penny with the emptiness of her home and her now-traumatized family. As they entered their military vehicle and departed the scene, Martha went to her friend's side and remained there for the next couple of days. It was crucial that she provide Penny

and her children the utmost of tenderness in their loss; a gentle hug, a warm embrace, a story read from a book to the children to keep the tragedy from constantly lingering in their thoughts.

For the next several days Martha devoted every moment of her time doing Penny's chores and preparing meals until her parents arrived to provide the assistance, love and comfort she needed during her time of loss.

The death of Penny's husband affected every family on the street. They all wanted the answers to the same questions Penny had asked of the Chaplin while at the same time fearing the answers. The pain and sorrow they would bring would be overwhelming. All of the families on base knew that any day the Chaplain could be visiting them to impart bad news. They prayed it would not be their doors he would knock on.

There were times I held Martha in my arms while she told me this story time and time again. But she also wanted me to know that she would always remember the good days, the best days of her life. Like the day she married me, the day our son was born and the day she received a letter from me disclosing to her that I would be coming home from Vietnam and that I was safe. No more waiting for War Department Letters. She was so happy then.

Martha had no choice. She would have to accept my orders as her new reality. She would have to take over as the matriarch of the family as I withdrew to the privacy of my office and eventually to the secret location where I would complete my mission. The military can be a cruel mistress.

CHAPTER 7

SEALED ORDER
CAPTAIN JASON E. RYAN 085960 USMC

Opening the manila envelope, I laid the contents from within on the top of my desk and began to read the bewildering pages of my next assignment. It was beyond belief. I asked myself why had I been chosen for this specialized unit and why the need for absolute concealment? I always thought that after completing my three-year tour of duty as a flight instructor at Pensacola my next duty station would be an assignment as a pilot to an active CH 46 Squadron stationed either on the east or west coast. I was anticipating a return to Okinawa with my family and to fly out of Marine Corps Air Station Futenma.

The war in Vietnam had been over for some time and the United States as far as I knew had departed the last of our outposts and troops with little fanfare. Hundreds of our service personnel had little chance of remaining overseas at a far eastern base with all the cutbacks. Most of our troops had already rotated home to their new duty stations. The only Marine bases I knew to be fully operational were MCAS Futenma and Iwakuni, Japan.

Headquarters Marine Corps had drawn up special orders for 14 H34 pilots. I couldn't believe it. The H34 had been retired from service in the Marine Corps for several years and replaced with more advanced

CH46s. Why were they assembling only H34 pilots and where were they going to find the "old dog"? As far as I knew they were all eventually sold, scrapped or cocooned somewhere in Arizona at our nation's aircraft boneyard.

Every individual that was chosen as a member in this group were unknown to each other except for one. I knew a Marine Captain by the name of Glen Thomas. The two of us had approximately the same date of rank and briefly served together. I assumed he received identical orders and would remember me from when we were Marine Aviation Cadets (MARCADs) assigned to VT-5, the training unit that was responsible for the introduction and completion of our carrier qualifications at NAS Barin Field, Foley, Alabama.

As students we agonized through a very difficult syllabus or segment of flight training in an attempt to receive our Commission and be designated a Naval Aviator. Our brief schedule at the Naval Air Training Command, NAS Pensacola, was the only time Captain Thomas and I were members of the same squadron or unit and our paths never crossed from that point on... until now.

Continuing to examine my orders I saw the names of eight qualified crew chiefs that were extraordinary mechanics and eight highly decorated crewmembers that had been straphangers or gunners on the H34 during the Vietnam War.

In the event of an illness or an unanticipated accident involving and injuring members of the primary flight crews there would be alternates to step in as their replacements. Four supplementary pilots, two crew chiefs and two straphangers were assigned to the group

as substitutes. In all the biographies I read I learned that every one of these Marines had flown over 50 missions in Vietnam during the 1968 Tet Offensive in the CH46s... not the H34's. Tet was one of the costliest periods in loss of life to our servicemen.

The officer selected to Command this assemblage of men was a Lt. Colonel and the Executive Officer was a Major. Officer's identities, biographies and histories were excluded from the contents of my orders, which stated that we would be introduced at some point prior to opening our training at Camp Pendleton. The unit's name or identification would be designated when training began in earnest during the middle of November. Surprisingly, these Marine pilots and the reserve crews would celebrate the Marine Corps Birthday together on November 10th and bond as a unit at that time.

CHAPTER 8

CAMP PENDLETON
SECRET OPERATIONS

L eaving my family, NAS Saufley and the Pensacola area was
 trouble-free yet my heart ached. With an uncertain future staring
me in the face, I was leaving all that was familiar. It was hard to
know that my students would be left behind to work with unfamiliar
instructors. But that's life… and this would be a lesson for of change
for us all.

Unexpected and new circumstances for the betterment of the Corps
would and could be expected at some point during their time in
service and it happened to them prematurely in their careers. It's
similar to battle plans. Once you fire the first shot from your rifle you
can throw away all the operational road maps and battle plans. You're
on a new path.

Accepting Top Secret Orders wasn't something I expected,
especially at this point in my career. This would be the first time that
Headquarters Marine Corps had given me an assignment that was
like being asked to enter a dark cave blindfolded and kill the beast
hiding inside. On the 5th of November, we who had been assigned to
the mission would collectively learn who the beast was and where it
was hiding.

I drove through the main gate at Camp Pendleton at 2135 hours on November 3rd, two days early and went directly to the Bachelor Officers Quarters to get a temporary room assignment. Locating the BOQ on base and checking in at the main desk I found the cost of the room was two dollars per day; for that stipend I'd receive a room that was approximately 8 x 10, a rack (bed), a pine desk with a chair, an end table with a single lamp, a chest of drawers and a private head (toilet) and shower.

A telephone hung on the wall next to the desk within easy reach. The phone could only be used for calls on the base, but it had a supplemental restricted outside line. Anyone wanting to use it for an outside call had to have a special card that when inserted into a slot at the base of the phone would give authorization to the cardholder to make a call anywhere in the world. Such a card had been inserted in my packet of special orders. I didn't know if I'd have cause to ever use it, but it was good to know.

Once settled in my room I took a quick shower and shave, fell down on my rack and put in about eight hours of uninterrupted sleep. The trip west had been a grueling trip that sapped every ounce of energy I had from me and the pain in my back was killing me after sitting hour after hour, watching the white line that ran down the middle of the road. It had an almost hypnotic effect.

Officers who were passing through the area and needed a place to hang their hats had a fairly nice room to use while transferring from one duty station to another at a rock bottom price. The accommodations were rather drab in color, but you couldn't beat the price.

Morning came too early as the sun streamed in through the window to wake me. My eyes greeted it with pain, but my soul greeted it with hope. The intensity of the light held a promise of a bright and successful day. It wasn't quite a guarantee that all would be okay in this mission, but there was a certain comfort in the warmth of the sunlight. Knowing I had about 22 hours free from duty I decided to familiarize myself with the base.

To begin my day I headed to the Officers Mess Hall for morning chow. Typical of all mess halls, it offered buffet-style service and long tables covered with red and white-checkered tablecloths. Soon I had run through the line, filling my tray with eggs over medium, fried potatoes and rye toast for a very reasonable price of just $1.25. I also paid 5 cents for a cup of coffee, which included all the refills I could handle free of charge. The day was starting out well.

A few officers were seated at the tables, but I didn't know a soul in the whole group. They were all infantry officers and they seldom came into contact with Marine Aviators. Our only connection or slightest interaction was when they were being taken on a mission in one of our helos or being picked up by us on a rescue. In their eyes, we were beneath them. Funny how they allowed us to save their lives, yet declined to give us the respect we deserved.

A few Grunts were seated at the far corner of the mess hall and I thought this might be a way to make some new friends. I headed to where they were seated and asked if I could join them.

"How about letting an aviator join you for breakfast?"

They nodded their approval and pointed to an open seat. The conversation went well for a while but when they asked, "Do they have any physically fit guys in the air wing?"

I knew they were ribbing me, but their words began to ruffle my feathers a bit. I'd have to give it back to them or they'd think I was a pushover. "Maybe you can press 200 pounds, but the mush between your ears puts you in a much lower category in regard to IQ. As I remember it, infantry officers must have at least an IQ of 100 and enlisted men a minimum of 85. The Air Wing requirements are considerable higher than infantry and for that reason gentlemen ------- you're walking and I'm riding." All this was bullshit but I didn't care.

I shot them a wink and a half-smile before continuing.

"I hope you never get lost in the bush and need some bright, witty and well-groomed Dapper Dan to find your confused ass because you can't read a compass and the enemy is pushing you to the limit and you need an emergency evacuation. Oh, by the way, thanks for the invite. Enjoyed chatting with you."

With that I got up and left my dirty tray in front of them adding, "How about cleaning up my mess and returning this dirty tray to the cleaning belt; that is one of the basic duties of an individual with the IQ of 100 isn't it?"

Leaving the Mess Hall I got into my car and continued my base-scouting adventure. Camp Pendleton was enormous in size; much larger than I expected. I went from the Exchange, where you could buy anything from bubble gum to beachwear and then to the base

hospital. Throughout the hundreds of acres on base there were shopping centers, libraries, uniform shops and gas stations. Even the Golden Arches of McDonald's had its place on the grounds.

From soccer fields to uniform shops, from food to recreation, the Marines here had everything they needed without having to leave base or government property. Since I had been in aviation my entire career I recognized the two entities were undeniably diverse in their mission. They were training in Ground Operations; we were in Air Operations.

I decided I had one more stop to make. I needed to go to the flight line and squadron area of HMM 374. It was the unit I was attached to while in Vietnam before transferring to Pensacola as a flight instructor.

The moment I walked into the Ready Room I recognized a junior captain by the name of Dale Newburg. Except for the scar on his left cheek – courtesy of a wound he received in Vietnam when he was called on to rescue a squad of Marines who'd been cut off from their main outfit – he looked the same as the last time I saw him. Dale's distinctive mannerisms, facial expressions and the inability to sit still for any length of time were still apparent.

When he saw me Dale rushed over and threw his arms around me. I think it shocked both of us, but that's how it is sometimes when you see a comrade in arms among a sea of strangers. Tears came to his eyes. He had total recall of the evening he crashed in rugged terrain and I was the only one in the area that would come to his rescue.

I remembered that day pretty well, too. In Dale's May Day call he said his aircraft was tangled in the trees on the side of a sheer cliff with no way for him or his crew to get out without putting themselves in further danger. They had to stay put until there was someone brave enough came to their rescue. That someone was yours truly.

My co-pilot was a brown bar (2nd Lt.), Lt. Robert Norman, who had just arrived in country and kept asking me over and over via the intercom, "Are you sure we ought to be doing this? Are you sure we ought to be doing this? How are we ever going to find them in this weather? Aren't you afraid of running into a mountain in all this rain and restricted visibility?"

Finally I snapped, "Shut the fuck up and listen. You're irritating me! You're my co-pilot, and you're building yourself a real poor reputation here. If it were you out there hanging by a thread wouldn't you want someone to come get your ass? Before you leave Nam you'll get used to what we're doing today; it's just routine. I might add, if you don't show some balls on the QT, when we get back to the base the Crew Chief and Gunner will tell all the guys in the squadron that the new guy is a PUSSY!"

That shut him up. Not another word came from his lips. I guess I gave him something to chew on.

We were heading over to pick Dale up, no questions asked. It was our duty. It was raining throughout the entire area with a heavy thunderstorm and downpour exactly where he went down. Lightning strikes in the area made things almost impossible, but we were going

to give it a good try. I slowed the aircraft down to a crawl moving along the terrain as guardedly and prudently as possible.

We were having difficulty finding him with the visibility being less than a mile but both Dale and I had ADF (Automatic Direction Finders) radios onboard and we used them as locators. He keyed his microphone and I just followed the head of my navigation needle to find him hanging there on the side of the cliff by a breath and a prayer in a driving rain.

After finding Dale's aircraft perched on the side of that cliff, I was astonished to see it hanging by the right main landing gear strut. Entangled by vines and branches, it couldn't hold much longer. I wondered how long before it would tumble down the mountainside. I couldn't delay getting into position so we could challenge what appeared to be impossible. This rescue was going to be unreasonably treacherous.

I moved my aircraft into a hover about 30 feet above what used to be Dale's H34. I radioed Dale that the only movement in the aircraft allowed would be the individual being hoisted up by my crew chief on the winch. Everyone else had to remain absolutely still. I told Dale to instruct his men that all they were allowed to do was maintain a normal breathing rhythm. I couldn't imagine what Dale's men were thinking. My hands were sweating and I wasn't the one being rescued!

Using the aircraft's winch to pull Dale's men up one by one from the crash site I held a steady hover. My Crew Chief received all the credit for pulling the four men of the downed crew as well as the squad

of Marines he had rescued just minutes before to the safety of my aircraft. I wrote him up for the Bronze Star for accepting a challenge.

Dale remembered that stormy night I came to his rescue after the engine in his aircraft failed. He kept telling me he owed me something, but I told him I knew he'd do the same for me. His tears said it all.

Our conversation lead to additional missions we had flown together. Missions good and bad. It was a surprise to listen to him, hear the wonderful things he had accomplished since returning to the states and that he was going to make the Marine Corps his career. I wished him luck and parted ways. He pointed me in the direction of the Commanding Officer's Office along with a "Semper Fi, Marine… Semper Fi."

Walking down a long passageway I came to the door that read "Lt. Colonel William A. Riddle, Commanding Officer HMM 374."

Knocking on the door, I waited until I heard the words, "Enter, stand easy and speak." Inhaling deeply, I stepped into the room.

Beau, the call sign he used when he was the senior ranking Major in 374 while serving in Vietnam, Lt. Colonel Riddle was shocked when he saw who it was that had just entered his office. It was good to see a familiar face.

We chatted for 30 minutes before we parted ways with the promise to meet at the O Club at 1700 hours.

That night was the first in a moon's age that I got drunk with a war buddy. The bullshit stories got larger than life as we poured drink after drink down our gullets. Before long we started to laugh. It was preposterous to think we had accomplished all those hazardous missions without being killed or at least critically injured.

I asked Beau, "How long have you been the CO of 374?"

"Long enough to know that all the paperwork is a pain in the ass," he said looking down at the bar. "About all I want to do now is take to the air and get away from it all. I wish I were a 1st Lt. again and had a 2nd Louie as my co-pilot... Then we could just fly along about 20 feet above the beach or chase coyotes out in the desert." With that he patted me on the back before picking up his glass to take another snort.

"Here's to it!" we said in unison. We knew we had a nasty hangover coming to us in the morning!

CHAPTER 9

RENDEZVOUS POINT

The 5th of November came quickly. With it came more anxiety and apprehension than I ever remember feeling before. I knew I was about to meet the Deputy Commander, U. S. Marine Corps Forces Special Operations, Brigadier General Paul Gardner, in the flesh. This General held in his hand a lot of men's futures in the Corps. He could crush a man's destiny and all his dreams in a heartbeat. Just the thought of Gardner sent chills running up and down my spine.

From the moment I first read my orders and the internal documents inserted within I knew that this group of pilots and support personnel were about to be given a task very much out of the ordinary. I identified it as an unremitting and challenging mission beyond human comprehension.

Why had my name been placed on this directory along with the names of all these distinguished Marines? I served my country well in both peace and war, but what caught the eye of Headquarters Marine Corps to focus in on me to stand beside these reverent officers and men? I assumed all of us were equally valuable to this mission that would take place in the not-too-distant future.

My fitness reports suggested I was admired by my former COs (Commanding Officers). While I carried the rank of 2nd Lieutenant through Captain, my Commanding Officers had placed me in the top five of all the officers holding the same rank in the squadrons in which I had been attached. Written in the comments section they remarked that they would be most pleased to have me in their squadron at a later date and that I would be one of their first choices if my name happened to be on an open availability list.

The only other qualification in my Service Record Book (SRB) that I could think of that might draw their attention to me was that I had earned the Silver Star, the Vietnamese Cross of Valor (a foreign award) and had fired a record 248 out of a 250 firing the M1 Rifle during my initial qualification in weapons training. Other than that I was just a standalone U.S. Marine serving his country that had received a couple medals for being at the wrong place at the right time.

After completing recruit training, the Commanding Officer of the 3rd Battalion at Parris Island attempted to send me to sniper school, but I had orders to pilot training as a Marine Aviation Cadet at Pensacola, Florida and desperately wanted to be an officer and pilot. I didn't want anything to do with being a sniper. Crawling around in the bush all covered with grass and weeds wasn't my idea of a comfortable field uniform. I signed up for pilot training and that's the MOS (Military Occupation Specialty) I wanted written after my service identification number.

I sat down long enough to write Martha and Kirk a short note to tell them I was fine and everything was going the Marine way. Hot and heavy.

The date and time finally arrived for me to seek out the stealthy location of where this team was to eat, sleep, train and live. Jumping into my car and hitting the gas it didn't take me long before finding the training center where I had been ordered to report. Immediately before leaving the BOQ I burned the pages of the entire manuscript as ordered and directed… all except page 23a. I committed to memory several of the items contained within the package; the rendezvous point was one of them.

General Gardner's private and very quiet living quarters and Administrative Offices were located on the eastern slopes of Camp Pendleton at least ten miles from highway 5 and the main entrance to Camp Pendleton. This secluded and out-of-the-way camp was a restricted area surrounded by chain-link fencing, barbed wire and military police with war dogs walking the enclosure throughout the grounds day and night. If you were invited you could enter. If you entered uninvited and you took it upon yourself to cross or climb the wire it was obvious you were going to be in what we Marines called "Deep Shit right up to the chin." From what I understood, war dogs if their handlers directed them to attack, would eat an intruder alive. I wouldn't want to test that theory.

Arriving at the location designated in my orders I parked my car in the makeshift lot adjacent to the main complex. Off to my left was a guard shack about the size of a phone booth painted in the Marine colors of red and yellow. An MP (Military Policeman) was seated inside. This particular Marine wasn't just any Marine; he looked more like a gorilla than a Marine.

He was enormous in size. It was pretty clear that in his spare time he lifted a lot of weights. His shirt looked as if it was about four sizes too small and was about ready to rip open with any movement or change in position he might make. As I approached this gorilla of a man he held up his right hand and ordered, "Halt! Come to a complete stop and identify yourself!"

No argument from me. This guy was twice as large as me and had a war dog sitting at the ready waiting for his attack command.

I uttered the code word designated in the briefing papers. "Taxpayer." Then I gave my last name, "Ryan." It was surreal as I stood frozen in place just 20 feet from the gate. Time ticked by in slow motion.

After checking the roster on a clipboard that hung inside the guardhouse the MP told me where to go and which room I needed to get to upon entering one of several buildings located off to my right.

Nestled among several oak trees, the structure had a red door and was located about 200 yards from the main gate. There were no pathways leading up to the building or its entrance; just paths made by people walking through the tall grass that surrounded the structure.

The building was about 50′ x 100′ and was built of used orange bricks. I didn't see any windows. At one end there was an oversized doorway that was painted red and from what I could tell there were escape hatches at the midpoint on both sides. Without any identification numbers, titles or signs for identification, no one would or could know what was taking place within the walls of this building. A quick shudder ran through my body as I pushed onward.

Affixing a sign with the unit or command in which they were serving identifies most buildings on Marine or Naval Bases. This was the only structure I had ever seen on a base that was void of any signs as to who was attached to this unit or what their training might be. This only served to add to my apprehension.

The MP handed me a backpack and relayed to me that the information inside was vital to whatever was to take place in Room 172. A final customary hand salute from the Corporal and I was on my way. The dog, on the other hand, never took his eyes off me until I was well out of reach of the MP.

Entering the building I walked about 20 paces down the passageway until I found the door marked '172' on my right. The passageway was just a flat gray color with nothing on the walls. Opening the door marked by a brass plate with '172,' I saw a mix of both officers and enlisted men dressed in their formal winter green uniforms.

Everyone was filling each other in on their identities, their former duty stations and when they had served in Vietnam. (A general question/answer/introduction period). The most noteworthy subject matter was why they had been selected for this specific operational unit. The common denominator was the H34. They all had previously flown them as pilots, crewed them as crew chiefs or were gunners on them during the Vietnam War.

Scarcely having time to introduce myself the door opened and in walked Brigadier General Gardner. Trailing behind were three men: a Lt. Colonel, a Major and a Gunny carrying an easel.
Someone yelled, "Attention on deck!"

The General replied, "At ease... take your seats."

At that moment everyone knew that this Colonel and Major were our new CO and Exec. We took our seats as ordered.

All four of the men could be genetic copies of one another. Each stood about six feet tall, weighing 180 to 200 pounds and each carried that rugged look expected of a high-ranking office with years of experience. On the left hand side of each uniform shirt, just above the pocket, were pinned into place several rows of ribbons. Above the ribbons were coveted gold Naval Aviator Wings. Every individual in that room had either Naval Aviator Wings or Wings designating them as flight crewmembers earned as a Crew Chief or Straphanger/ Gunner. At one time or another all had flown in combat and had given his all for his fellow Marines and country.

CHAPTER 10

INTRODUCTION
X.O.

General Gardner set in motion the introduction of our new CO, Lt. Colonel Dwayne Holiday. Until most recently and upon being selected to command HMM Joshua – our new unit – Holiday had been the Commanding Officer of a CH46 squadron stationed and training out of the Marine Corps Air Station, Tustin, California.

He had served two tours in Vietnam, one as Executive Officer of a H34 squadron... or second in command. It was while on his second tour in Vietnam he became the CO of a CH46 squadron by reason of the untimely death of the squadron's leadership. His CO had been killed attempting to rescue a team of Recon Marines that had been observing NVA Troops along the Ho Chi Minh Trail. What made the rescue so challenging was that the Recon Marines had been sighted by the NVA and were running for their lives to reach the assigned pickup zone, which was called LZ Potpie.

Making contact with the team via radio, the helicopter aircraft commander, who was Colonel Holiday's former CO, told the team leader, Corporal Gonzalez, that there was a clearing about half a click ahead next to a riverbed. They'd pick the Marines up there. When Team Eagle Eye arrived at the edge of the extraction point hidden

in the tree line, they passed the word to the circling helo that the LZ appeared to be cold.

Gonzalez passed the word saying, "No enemy activity or small arms fire."

Holiday's CO began his approach to a landing. All hell broke loose upon touching down, with both the CO and his co-pilot killed within seconds. Surrounded and outnumbered 10 to one, the Crew Chief and Straphanger had little choice but to surrender. Escape was impossible. They dropped their weapons and threw their arms in the air as an enactment of surrender.

Recalling their former briefings the rest of the crew knew NVA soldiers were brutal to prisoners. Capture was definitely out of the question if escape was conceivable. From a distance Corporal Walters, the sniper attached to Team Eagle Eye, watched as the enemy tied the crewmembers' hands behind their backs and forced them to their knees. When a NVA Officer withdrew his sword, getting ready to behead the captives, Walters without hesitation shot and killed the bastard.

The Recon Team was compelled to engage the enemy to stop the beheading. As a result four members of the team were killed; only one escaped. It was Corporal Walters. He made his way through the jungle to the alternate LZ and was picked up by a Marine Chopper later that day just before dark.

With the death of his Skipper, Col. Holiday as second in command was automatically promoted to CO and continued to hold that

position of authority for the remainder of his time in country with HMM 361. Corporal Walters is in this room at this time and a member of our newly formed unit.

General Gardner announced, "Cpl. Walters, would you please stand up?"

This was followed by a round of applause so loud that it could be heard out at the guard shack.

It was at this point General Gardner changed the procedure of introduction. He requested that, beginning in the front row and from left to right, each individual stand up, introduce himself to the unit, tell them of their combat tours, what medals they were awarded, etc. Each man was to give a general description of himself, what part of the U.S. he came from and the aircraft he flew while in Vietnam.

We each took our turn. We were also told that if we had any difficulty accepting this assignment and if we wanted to be discharged from this obligation we would be without any questions asked.

The only thing that General Gardner said in closing was, "If you decline this mission your Marine Corps career is over." Gruffly, he added, "You will be also restricted to this compound, you will be relieved of all duties and you will not have access to any telephones for correspondence to anyone until this mission is complete. It will look as if you have disappeared from the face of the earth." Looking around the room, he barked, "Any questions?"

Greeted by total silence, General Gardner said, "CC, you have the floor."

The new Executive Officer, Major Charles Canyon, call sign "CC," began his introduction. He presented himself as a soft-spoken gentle giant that everyone took to immediately. His voice was soft and clear as he addressed everyone in the room that it felt as if he were our father who was offering advice and concern. CC was easy to trust.

He told us, "Get your Wills and Irrevocable Trusts up to date, and any other legal documents that have to or must be upgraded. Most of all, do not forget any of your family members."

Everyone in the room bonded with him instantly because it was obvious that he took a personal interest in not only us but also each and every member of our family. He was an individual you liked with certainty and beyond a shadow of a doubt.

CC was one of the most highly decorated officers in the Corps. Major Canyon had not just one but two Navy Crosses awarded for action above and beyond the call of duty.

The General felt compelled to interrupt CC to tell us his knowledge of a mission CC flew during his tour in Vietnam. It had to be told before continuing with the introductions as the men had to know the character of their leadership.

He shared one of CC's missions where two Army Helos attached to the 101st Airborne based out of Pleiku had been shot down, were fiercely engaged with the enemy and fighting for their lives.

As the story goes, Major Canyon and his wingman happened to be in the area flying along fat, dumb and happy on what we Marines call a milk run delivering supplies to an outpost in the A Shau Valley. The A Shau Valley runs inland from the coastal city of Hue, to and along the border of Laos. To the NVA the valley was a critical sanctuary from where the communist could launch attacks into Vietnam from Laos.

Both Huey gunships, Dugan 1 and Dugan 2, were cruising at altitude looking for targets of opportunity when they found a column of trucks filled with troops moving southward on the Ho Chi Minh Trail. Without hesitation Dugan 1 started his run firing at the lead truck.

He had just started his run when his aircraft was hit by what must have been an RPG or Rocket-Propelled Grenade. With his aircraft whirling around in circles, Lt. Higgens, the Aircraft Commander, attempted everything possible to stop the rotating and spinning but ultimately crashed in a shallow riverbed about 1500 meters from the enemy.

His wingman witnessed the crash and without hesitation started in for the rescue. While inbound on the approach the copilot was mortally wounded, taking a round to the throat, and the pilot was hit in the right leg above the knee and the right arm between the elbow and shoulder. Both wounds shattered the bones in the arm and leg, making it impossible to fly the aircraft. His aircraft crashed a short distance from his wingman. Both the gunner and crew chief were uninjured in the crash.

Assisting the flight crew from the cockpit area the gunner and crew chief came under intense enemy fire. Once safely out and away

from the aircraft without injuries they began dragging both the pilot and co-pilot along in the shallow water with what ammunition and weapons they could carry toward Lt. Higgins and his crew.

Suddenly and with little warning, two NVA soldiers jumped out of the brush and began to fire their AK47s in the men's direction. Before they could hit their mark Sgt. Thomas, the crew chief from Dugan 1, shot and killed both NVA soldiers. Without hesitation Thomas threw his weapon over his shoulder, grabbed the ammunition they had been carrying and as rapidly as he could run joined up with the rest of the men from Dugan 1.

Lt. Higgins, the senior officer on the ground, placed in motion a series of commands that set up a field of fire that would provide them their best chance of survival until the Marine crew who had responded to their call could arrive.

General Gardner continued with his narrative.

"CC, your executive officer, responded to their call and without hesitation diverted his aircraft to the coordinates he received minutes earlier. On the way he briefed the gunner and crew chief to what would or could be expected when they arrived at the crash scene. He said, "the zone is hot, the area is saturated with enemy troops and we're going in alone. Expect the worse!'

"Hearing the sounds of the helos as they approached his position Lt. Higgins desperately called out over his radio, 'BROKEN ARROW, BROKEN ARROW.'"

We all knew that this call is used when desperate and urgent help is required to alert anyone and everyone in the area that the outfit or unit calling is in urgent need of help and need all personnel within striking distance to come to their aid.

The General continued. "They were about to be overrun. Within minutes two Navy A4 attack aircraft from the USS Independence were making runs on the enemy positions that Lieutenant Higgins had marked with smoke bombs.

"The lead A4 directed CC Holliday and his wingman in their helos to climb to 4000 feet and remain east of the target area till further notice. Watching the skill with which the A4s made their runs CC was in awe, amazed by how quickly they made waste of the enemy trucks and the immediate surrounding area.

"Lt. Higgins on the ground had radio contact with the A4 pilots on guard frequency, a frequency that was only to be used when calling 'BROKEN ARROW' or someone was in unfathomable distress. They passed the word that they were ready for the extract and that the enemy fire had diminished considerably.

The General wore a somber expression as he continued his retelling of CC's adventure. "Calling the helos, the lead A4 pilot called, 'Marine 1… Marine 2, this is Scrambler one do you read?' CC replied, 'Roger, that's affirmative.' The pilot said, "after our next pass you are cleared off the perch for the extraction. Make your entry from north to the south. We'll make our runs on the east and west side of you during the extract. Depart to the south. Do you copy?' CC replied with a 'Roger.' The A4 pilots climbed to a safe altitude, positioning their

aircraft to make their run abeam of the helo. CC came off the perch and headed inbound toward the LZ!"

The General seemed pretty excited to tell CC's story. "While inbound on the approach there were enemy rounds hitting his aircraft and tracers coming from every heading on the compass. CC's crew knew without any doubt they were at the right place at the wrong time.

"Landing at this particular LZ was not in the plan of the day. CC was supposed to be delivering chickens, pigs and foodstuff to Camp Angel... not drawing enemy fire while making an unexpected pickup of two-downed Army helo crews."

The General shot a look at CC and nodded.

"Landing in the shallow riverbed round after round kept striking the aircraft, the smell of cordite lingered in the cabin and cockpit as the Crew Chief and Straphanger kept firing in hopes of keeping the enemy from overrunning their position while they made the pick-up."

"Running from every position imaginable, everyone from the down crews was either aiding the wounded or targeting the enemy with their weapons until we had all hands aboard from both down crews."

CC picked up where the General left off. The General would let him tell his own tale.

"Sitting in the cockpit with Plexiglas as the only thing between me and the enemy as we waited for all the downed personnel to get aboard was the most dangerous time of the extraction. All I could do

was sit there with my mind running wild. I knew an enemy soldier was lining me up in the crosshairs of his rifle. That NVA soldier was doing his best to squeeze off a round that would kill me."

The General picked the story back up there. "As he sat there, adrenalin rushing through his body and his heart pounding, CC knew that he would be up and out of the zone in at least 60 seconds. He lived that event, he visualizes it to this day. This particular incident will remain in his memory for the rest of his life."

The General told us that during the extraction both Major Holiday's gunner and crew chief were wounded, three pilots were dead from Dugans 1 and 2, and Holiday was wounded in the calf of his left leg. All WIA, KIAs and the remaining crew members made it out. No one was left behind. Other than that, it was listed and printed in his CC's logbook as a milk run.

The Award Committee had written on the After Action Report seven words: ABOVE AND BEYOND THE CALL OF DUTY. The Navy Cross would come months later to all members of the flight crew for that particular mission.

CHAPTER 11

MARCAD FRIEND
A DISMISSAL OF ANOTHER

One by one, every man present had taken the microphone in hand, walked up to the podium and gave his name, rank, serial number and a brief resume about who he was, his family, schools he attended – both civilian and military – former duty stations and where he had served.

One of the first to stand after CC was a Major Kenneth Forest. He spoke freely and candidly as he told us that after the war ended in Vietnam he had been rotated stateside to the Marine Corps Air Station El Toro, California. At El Toro he was to transition from Helos to F4s, fixed-wing fighter aircraft.

He let everyone in the room know he was quite happy with his previous assignment flying the Phantom. He also let it be known he wasn't particularly on Cloud Nine with this most recent assignment, but that he would do his best to endure whatever the Marine Corps wanted him to do.

With the words "do his best to endure" barely out of his mouth General Gardner interrupted him. "Major, you are dismissed and are to follow Sgt. Strickland from this room."

We were all stunned. We never saw Major Forest again.

General Gardner made his point early as he had been waiting in the background for this moment. Anyone dissatisfied with this assignment would be discharged and discontinued as a member of the group. Major Forest was immediately labeled a weak link in the chain who couldn't be counted on with total commitment.

Of all the men who would introduce themselves, the one person I was most interested in hearing from was Captain Glenn Thomas. Where he had been and where had he had served was a surprise to me and to almost everyone in the room.

Captain Thomas had two tours of duty in Vietnam and flew over 100 missions all over what we called "I Corps" or the most northern area of South Vietnam. In doing so he had been awarded one Navy Cross, one Silver Star and one DFC, along with several awards from the Vietnamese Government. He was one of the most decorated individuals in the room. I might add he also appeared to be the most unassuming and respectful human being in this gathering of men.

It wasn't long before it was Captain Thomas's turn to take the floor. He introduced himself, tapping the microphone to make sure it still worked well, and without faltering asked his fellow Marines why he was standing in room 172 filled with the best of the best that the Corps had to offer. He told us that he was of the opinion that he was somewhat equal in likeness to many that spoke before him and hoped they would accept him for who he was and what he stood for. He was a Marine through and through. He added that he would defend us, his brothers in arms, until his last breath.

Several others stood up and made their intros. Overall, their reputations and temperaments were surprisingly similar to each and every one of us in the room. We truly were brothers in arms.

With introductions completed, General Gardner took the lead by saying, "Open the backpacks given to you upon entering the compound. Take out the map that is in its waterproof jacket."

In doing so we found a map of French Indo China printed and published in the 1940s. An overlay of Cambodia, Laos and present-day Vietnam was provided inside one of the folds. The map was insignificant; it was the overlay that was of material importance. It contained two defined escape routes, emergency LZs for pick up, where emergency radios, food and water could be found, along an E & E (escape and evasion) trail. Instructions were included stating that this overlay will not and could not fall into enemy hands and must be destroyed if it was clear that we were going to be captured.

The Gunny that had carried the easel into room 172 then uncovered the hidden contents of the map. Without saying a word he then left the room. It was color charted with all the necessary info that was needed for an escape. We were told that we would receive up-to-date copies prior to our departure from Point Origin, our starting point, if need be.

The General then said, "Recon teams from the 3rd Reconnaissance Battalion out of Camp Butler, Okinawa, Japan have been in and out of North Vietnam conducting surveillance, identifying, observing, and placing materials, weapons and equipment along the trails of the two designated escape routes if you should need them. They are also

collecting information that will be forwarded to you when you've begun training in earnest. I might add their presence in Vietnam was detected several times by NVA soldiers yet dealt with swiftly and quietly by one of the team members and everything at this moment in time is still in our favor.

"The acting Vietnamese Government has been consistent and unwavering in saying they have returned all remaining captives or POWs to U. S. authorities prior to the 29 March 1973 deadline.

"Our Recon Teams have established that the Government of Vietnam has detained a small number of pilots, ground troops and people that have knowledge of sensitive material and weapons. These particular individuals are being held against their will in a prison camp located 50 miles to the north of the former DMZ and 10 miles due west from the coastline. The closest base to give aide to this NVA Prison Camp when it comes under attack from us is over 78 miles away.

"With the signing of the Paris Peace Agreement, Article 8 of that treaty prohibited the detention of any U.S servicemen or citizens beyond March 29, 1973. The mandatory exchange of all prisoners were to be made as soon as a satisfactory time and location could be arranged. Their word was and is useless rubbish."

The General looked really angry. He growled, "We have authenticated as many as 36 captives located in what we have designated Camp Jericho. Formerly these prisoners were listed as MIAs or KIAs in their respective services.

"The use of our recon teams out of Camp Butler have done a magnificent job in gathering the approximate number of detainees, where they are quartered within Camp Jericho and how many NVA troops are on guard duty on any given day and at any given moment. They have also determined what day of the week, the time of the day the enemy will be at their weakest and unable to thwart or successfully oppose a Strike Force entering their compound.

"We have positively identified these individuals or captives through the use of long-range photography equipment. We have hundreds of photographs taken while these men worked in the surrounding fields or walked the fence line of their respective camp. You are going to bring them home."

The General scanned the room.

"I will post a list of their names on the bulletin board for you to view. Perhaps you have a friend or someone you know that is on this list."

CHAPTER 12

INTRODUCTION OF THE COMMANDING OFFICER

General Gardner continued by saying that for the next three weeks each and every one of you will be given the assignment and duty of familiarizing yourselves with the men in this room. "You will know all hands completely, from their date of birth to the current calendar day. You will know each other as if you were educated in the same home and they were your brothers."

Turning away from the men seated in front of him, General Gardner called to Colonel Holiday to come forward. "Colonel Holiday, you and your Executive Officer, Major Canyon, will have eight weeks to prepare this group of men for their most challenging mission to date. They are the best of the best. Prepare them for the unknown. Ready them for this unusual and extraordinary mission. Bring home those that the enemy has failed to return to us. Col. Holiday, step forward and tell your men who you are. Bring them up to date as to what is in your combined futures."

Colonel Holiday began with a real upbeat tone to his voice. "First and foremost, welcome aboard. What an honor it has been to be chosen to command this group of men. After reading all your service records I'm not surprised the Commandant has chosen the code name for our

detachment to be identified by the code name "Joshua."

"You have been selected in part as a member of this unit because you will not and have never failed your fellow officers and men," continued Holiday. "Only your death will bring a climax to your commitment or assignment to duty. The norm for you in battle is to complete the mission without failure."

He eyeballed each of us. "To give you an idea of what is expected of you and your squadron personnel I have summed it up in the following sentence… This is going to be an extraordinarily dangerous mission for this group, one that I know will be brought to a successful conclusion."

The Colonel nodded his head as if to emphasize the clear and present danger of what we were about to undertake.

"You will be broken down into two teams. The 3rd Recon Battalion will brief you at a later date. They are on their way here at this very moment. You will garner from them the harvested material gleaned from their penetration into enemy territory. You will commit to memory the blueprints they have drawn up of Camp Jericho and the necessary escape routes you will need if you lose your aircraft inbound or outbound."

The Colonel paced back and forth slowly as he spoke.

"An exact building by building of the enemies Camp Jericho is under construction within this compound. Its completion will be absolute in the next few days. The dimensions of all the structures are

meticulously true to size. The internal design of these buildings are unknown, but we definitely know what shacks the enemy has been using for our troops as far as living quarters. We also know where the enemy spends most of their time and where they sleep.

"Everything from trees to garbage cans, heads, storage areas, I MEAN EVERYTHING being built in this compound will be the exact duplicate of the camp you will assault. When you arrive at Camp Jericho it will be like you have been stationed there for at least one tour of duty. Before you depart on this mission you will rehearse and rehearse the entry and attack on this compound a multitude of times. You will know where the enemy stands his watch and where he took his last breath.

"Four six-man rifle squads, with one member of the team an expert with the bow and arrow, are attached to the 3rd Reconnaissance Battalion. They have been ordered to eliminate all enemy personnel at a specific time and date.

"Our Sniper/Rifle Teams will be inserted into hostile territory 72 hours prior to your arrival by the use of the USS Sunfish, a naval submarine. At exactly two miles off shore they will transfer from the Sunfish to rubber rafts and make their way to the beach.

"Their drop-off point is environmentally friendly to us, void of the enemy, and the area is completely unpopulated so as to avoid detection. Their obstacles are the jungle and the mountains. The 72 hours will allow the team time to bypass all obstacles in their pathway to Camp Jericho. This early entry will also put them in position to accomplish the most important portions of the operation:

1. Eliminate the unsuspecting guards using silent weapons;

2. Enter the compound undetected and assassinate the men on duty in the radioshack along with all their equipment;

3. Destroy all remaining radios.

4. Eliminate the remaining forces while they are at lights out in their quarters.

"When our Special Ops Aircraft, code name 'Rat Trap,' makes contact with our Recon Teams via airborne radio and have scanned the skies for enemy aircraft… and determined all is clear and have received a report that our recon teams are in position and ready to engage the enemy, they will be given from Command the order: eliminate and terminate all opposing personnel."

It seemed as if Holiday would never take a breath. He spoke quickly and precisely.

"Aboard our LPH (Landing Platform Helicopter) Carrier our helo crews will be at their stations strapped in with their checklists completed and ready to go. Receiving and copying this same message from Rat Trap, they will start their engines, engage their rotors and depart for Jericho. By the time they depart the ship and fly the approximate 30-mile leg to Jericho the Landing Zones will be in Recon's hands."

Here he clapped his hands together to make a point.

"Again, the closest base with men and equipment that will be able to come to the aid of the NVA at Jericho is more than 78 miles north of your position. By vehicle averaging 45 miles per hour on rough road you will have 1 hour 45 minutes to finish the initial phase of your mission. We expect you to be in and out of Camp Joshua in 50 minutes – no more. By then you should be on course to the comfort of the Princeton.

"Additional Information will come later as we get deeper into the training portion of this operation. I'm getting a little ahead of myself. I'm sorry, I just wanted you to know what is in the future and the demands that are about to be placed on your shoulders. In the meantime, Gunny Strickland, a member of the 3rd Recon Battalion who you have seen passing around material throughout this briefing, will be going with the vanguard as a member of one of the six-rifle teams on the initial insert when we receive the word to go.

"In my assessment of Gunnery Sergeants in the Corps, he is the best. He has had three tours of duty in Vietnam and has the Navy Cross and two Silver Stars for bravery under the most adverse conditions. He also has two purple hearts for wounds received in battle."

Giving a quick nod to Strickland, the Colonel continued.

"He will be assigning you your living quarters and a roommate before this day is over. Oh, has anyone decided he wants to be relieved of this assignment?"

Here he paused. Silence was the answer.

"Is there anyone who wants to spend the next several months in isolated lockdown and be treated as if he has an infectious disease?"

Again, he looked around the room.

Not a single person uttered a syllable or raised his hand. Col. Holiday, our new CO responded. "I didn't think so. Semper Fi."

CHAPTER 13

H34 TRAINING BEGINS

Not long after that day of introduction, Major "CC" Canyon, started in on our training. After a short hello and welcome aboard, he filled us in with some of the blanks concerning the use of the H34 instead of the CH46.

He explained, "The H34 had less problems with maintenance, had dimensions that would fit into smaller LZs, could take more hits with less damage than the CH46 and everyone on this team has more than 1000 hours in both the right or left seat."

He added, "As for the aircraft assigned to the Joshua Teams, they were most recently manufactured at the Morton, Pennsylvania, plant and provided to the Corps by Boeing Vertol Aircraft Division for this mission. The Marines Corps at this time do not have current NATOPS (Naval Air Training Ops) personnel training H34 pilots or ground school instructors. We will have personnel employed by Boeing who for many years have taught systems and procedures in Sikorsky products as our instructors.

"All of our selected personnel will be transitioned into the H34 as Aircraft Commanders and will receive a minimum of 100 hours in type before our departure from the States. Warm-ups with multiple landings, auto rotations and all emergency procedures will be given and successfully completed prior to our departure from Camp Pendleton."

CC made sure we were listening.

"Listen up," he said. "A minimum of 10 carrier landings will be made using the flight deck of the USS Valley Forge. She will be just off the U.S Coast behind Catalina Island when carrier operations and re-qualifications begin. The ship will be visible to fishing boats that depart from Dana Point and Long Beach Harbors yet not an unusual sight for anyone observing the Valley Forge. The U.S. Navy has periodic exercises and operations in these waters so if fishing boats or yachts observe her on the west side of the island it won't be out of the ordinary."

We all nodded in response.

"The USS Valley Forge LPH 8 has a renowned and illustrious history," said CC. "From WW ll, Korea and then to Vietnam she has had on her deck everything from the F4U Corsairs to H34 Helicopters. She is an Essex Class Carrier, straight deck, 888 feet in length, has a top speed of 33 knots, holds 90-100 aircraft and has a crew of 3448 officers and men. Her battle ribbons are too many to list."

"The aircraft we are to use in this operation have already arrived at this compound. Sikorsky Check Airman and instructors from Sikorsky Aircraft Company flew them into our compound area two nights ago. Ground school on the aircraft will begin tomorrow for the pilot group in this building. Crew Chiefs and Gunners will be in the adjacent building with the orange doors in room 454."

"After our band of brothers gets to know one another, Col. Holiday and I will by, observance, select who will fly with whom and who will be the Search and Reserve Crew. Oh, yes, and the only difference in the aircraft you will be flying on this mission and the one you flew in Vietnam is the color. They are all painted dark green with white lettering."

He then directed us to get to know each other the way Marines do it best.

"The Officer/Enlisted Club, so to speak is where you will get to know one another. It has not been designated as an enlisted or an officer's club. Both ranks and rates will frequent the club, but bear in mind that there is a rank structure in the Corps. Remember where you stand. Drunkenness will not be accepted as an excuse for bad behavior and

insubordination will not be tolerated. Rank Has Its Privileges. Now, enjoy the free beer and booze, and let's get to know each other. For the moment you are free and clear of all responsibilities other than getting a roommate and moving into your new quarters."

At 1330 hours the Gunny lead the group to their new Officer/Enlisted Club. After about an hour of free drinks and without forewarning, one Corporal Benson (who had one too many alcoholic beverages) deliberately knocked over Captain O'Connor's drink. As the contents splashed all over his uniform O'Connor said, "You stupid ass! What the hell are you doing? I saw you intentionally knock over my drink with the intent of it spilling all over me. Corporal Benson get off that bar stool right now and stand at attention when I'm talking to you."

With that order Benson responded to Captain O'Connor with two simple words, "Fuck You."

That's all it took. O'Connor ordered him out of the club to his room and told him he could consider himself on report. The following morning General Gardner closed the club to all personnel for a period seven days. Benson was discharged from the unit.

I had to wonder if Benson had done what he'd done on purpose. Not everyone was cut out for such a challenging secret mission.

CHAPTER 14

RESTRICTIONS/ROOM ASSIGNMENTS/ BOOZE AND CHOW

Affter the commotion with Benson's antics died down Gunny Strickland finished the day by assigning everyone to a room. Strickland called me forward. By a stroke of luck Thomas and I were assigned to the same room. Shaking hands, he told me that he remembered me from the training command and that we were in the same group of Cadets that qualified on the carrier together . He said, "Hey, I think we hit the boat on the same day!" He remembered that after qualifying we were ordered by our instructors to the "O" Club at Mainside Pensacola for the standard Toast to Victory.

I remembered that event as well.

Meeting at the O Club as directed we were told that we were required to make a toast and drink a sabotaged cocktail our instructors called **"The Over-Boost,"** a large glass filled with a mixture of a variety of alcohols taken from each and every bottle that happened to be on the shelves at the Officers Club at that moment.

With a thimbleful of alcohol taken from every bottle on the shelf, the mixture of this "snake venom" was served to us in an enormous glass. After reaching the final bottle at the end of the last shelf Captain Redford turned to me.

"You are approaching the point where you will become a Naval Aviator," he announced loudly. "Congratulations! It is here and now that you will learn the meaning of a true over-boost."

With that, I was to take the glass, which was really an oversized Mason Jar and drink the entire contents all at once. The instructors looked on and laughed. These accessories in crime were good at poisoning Cadets while we participated in the time-honored Toast to Victory.

We drank, they laughed and we vowed revenge. It took a good 24 hours to feel normal again. I remember thinking I'd never be well again and that I'd give all my worldly possessions to feel better. Ah, the good ol' days.

Thomas didn't get his revenge, but I got mine. I took my time, but eventually my revenge came in the form of a syringe full of a strong laxative. I got the syringe from a Hospital Corpsmen and good friend. I put that laxative through the cork into the bottle of whiskey that I was required by tradition to give my instructor after hitting the boat. Every time he took a shot from that bottle I knew he'd get the runs. I wonder if he ever put two and two together. It gave me great pleasure to see this man down that whiskey, shot after shot. He hadn't been the best instructor. In fact, he was a bit of shit, so I gave him as good as he'd given me. I figured it was appropriate.

I thought about the incident. "Redford, you deserved it and I have no regrets!" My only prayers were where the runs would happen... I thought it would be great if it were while instructing a student in

his aircraft. I giggled to myself a little as I thought about that scene. Redford shitting his pants while airborne.

The following morning Colonel Holiday's voice called everyone in the group, to room 172 and ordered us to surrender the keys and registration papers of our vehicles. Forfeiting the keys and registration papers of our vehicles was easier said than done.

Holiday yelled, "Those of you who are married and have only one vehicle will have his car delivered to his wife/home/mother /father along with an official document from HQ Marine Corps telling them you have been immediately deployed and that you are unable to discuss where or when you will return."

He added, "It was stated in your orders to bring additional clothing and uniforms; hopefully you have done that. Oh, and getting back to your vehicles, anyone who is single will have his automobile impounded and placed in a storage facility here on the base until the day of his return. We are going to be that restrictive."

I remember thinking that without transportation our unit would be really limited as to what we could do in our free time. Without transportation the O/E Club would be our only recreation. We were told that if we left the compound that we'd be taken into custody and placed in the station brig only to be released after the conclusion of this mission. That was a mighty big restriction!

Once Gunny Strickland delivered his news he happily recorded the event in the company log, with time, place, name, and a picture of the VINs taken from our vehicles. I'll never forget the smile on his face.

DMV registration papers would prove ownership once we returned home, which would eliminate confusion around returning personal property to the proper owner. By taking our mode of transportation away the entire group was restricted to the compound without giving an order saying as much. However, we all understood the necessity. This was, after all, a secret mission... a very important mission.

The time was approaching 1200 hours when Gunny Strickland stepped forward to announce that lunch would be served in the Mess Hall and for everyone to follow him. Once inside an amazing up-to-date building we found an extravagant dining room that contained everything from A to Z. It had the finest of everything that would be needed for a larger-than-life dining experience. We were speechless. We weren't used to such extravagances. There were countless numbers of naval personnel who attended us and served our every need. It was a dream in living color for me.

The dining tables were covered with linens and set with the most expensive china and silverware that money could buy. It was as if we were about to be served by a renowned maître d' from Paris. In fact, there were two staff members serving every table/four to a table. What a treat! They wore naval uniforms without any insignia or rank on their sleeves and the name-tags all read the same last name: Smith. It was surreal.

A great variety of foods were on the menu with the finest of wines, both reds and whites. We were given the impression that the Brass gave little consideration in regard to cost. I looked at the others, wondering if they thought the same thing I did. Was this our last meal... the Marine's Last Supper?

After lunch and with time rapidly approaching 1300 hours, Sgt. Strickland sought our attention and told us to follow him. Once outside he pointed to two very large buildings. That is where we would find our assigned rooms. The enlisted men are billeted in the building on the left; the officer's quarters would be in the building on the right. Everyone was finally out of the BOQ or Marine Barracks.

Once inside, Glenn and I discovered our room wasn't just a room but rather a small apartment. It was without equal to anything I had ever seen for a BOQ room for any officer in all the years I had been in the Corps. Our assigned room was divided into three areas.

Entering the apartment placed you immediately into the living room, with a kitchen located to the far rear of the room. If you turned right you went into a private bedroom with a rack, a nightstand and a very large desk located at the far corner. It was the same if you went left. The sleeping quarters of your choice had a walk-in closet, plus its own shower and toilet facility. Separated as they were by the living room and kitchen gave the bedrooms a feeling of acceptable privacy.
The living room contained a couch, two small Lazy Boy recliners, two end tables with lamps and an overhead ceiling fan. Located on the extreme back wall or far end of the living room was a very small kitchen that was more like a bar that housed a refrigerator. We opened it to find that it was filled with snacks and beer. Glenn and I smiled at each other. Heaven without having to die!

On top of the fridge there were miniature bottles of alcoholic beverages from just about every brewery and spirit/whiskey maker in the world. We couldn't believe our eyes. A note on the bar that separated the kitchen from the living room told us not to worry about

field daying (cleaning) our apartment. We would have maid service to clean and straighten up our unit.

All we had to do was reach for the silver handle and flush the toilet. Wow, what a sendoff!

CHAPTER 15

TRAINING BEGINS

The following morning Glenn and I were up at 0630 hours, ate a hardy breakfast and went to area 1 to begin ground school on the H34. William Prentice and Frank Dawson, our Boeing/ Sikorsky Tech Reps, were already in the classroom awaiting our arrival.

Boeing assigned Prentice and Dawson to our unit as instructors to bring us up to date on aircraft systems and procedures. As FAA-Designated Ground School Instructors with flight and operational authority they were able to sign off any individual they deemed qualified as Aircraft Commanders in the Sikorsky UH34 as well as signing off pilots in other categories of aviation equipment. Their qualifications were without criticism.

Prentice and Dawson divided the group of pilots into two sections, with Prentice leading Section 1 and Dawson leading Section 2.

I had been assigned to Section 1. Thomas was in Section 2 with Dawson.

Prentice was a tiny, undersized slip of a man who stood about 5' 2" and weighed a maximum of 125 pounds. He was a highly regarded professional pilot that was proud of his background who had

remained pleasant and congenial throughout his aviation career. Right from the get-go Prentice requested all hands in his section to address him by his first name.

He said, "My name is Bill, and I think we should begin our program in a relaxed atmosphere in the classroom." Informally clad in a short-sleeve collared shirt, Bill spoke softly as he laid out the rules and expressed how important time was to us all.

He told us, "Your uniform of the day will be utilities, the Marine standard work uniform. Classes will commence precisely at 0800 hours every day. Supplies, manuals and materials needed for the days study would be on your desks upon arrival in the classroom, and I think it best you take the same seat in our assigned classroom each day. Each room is configured exactly the same, and now and again we will be in a different room, depending on the system we are studying or the procedure we are attempting to learn."

Bill was a no-nonsense guy. Straight away our class began with Bill introducing the basic dimensions, gross weights and speeds of the H34. Unknowingly we had completed the first two chapters of our two-volume instructional manuals within minutes. The information received came fast and furious. Without delay we were already on page 73, Power Plant, Chapter 5.

Chapter 5 was on the Wright R-1820-84, an engine that developed 1525hp (horsepower). The majority of our class remembered from ground schools past a good portion of the information Bill was passing out. I was sure while forming our unit the Joint Chiefs wanted all members in this unit to be former H34 pilots or crewmembers. The courses and systems could be accelerated with recall used as a vital aid in our ground school training classes. They were right.

The R-1820-84 was a gargantuan engine that was positioned forward and below the level of the pilots. Flying the H34 in Vietnam, I remember the engine had taken a lot of hits from enemy ground fire and blocked many of the rounds that would have entered the cockpit, which could have taken out a crew member during the most critical phase of flight. That is the approach and landing of the aircraft in the LZ (landing zone). If pilots were wounded on the approach it was usually to the buttocks or the back of the legs.

The class laughed when I said, "I sat on two flak jackets six inches deep to protect the family jewels."

Eventually maintenance put a quarter-inch piece of steel under both the HAC and co-pilots seat cushions.

The 1820, as we pilots called it, had a wide range of power settings and RPMs that had to be committed to memory. To accomplish an assortment of maneuvers and speeds to conclude a typical mission the squadron pilots used these settings.

We studied and went through the H34 panel by panel. First hydraulics, then flight instruments, electrical, fuel, instrument panel and finally on to the engine start and rotor engagement checklists. Our initial classroom studies lasted about four days with testing on Friday of the first week. I was surprised when everyone passed. Eighty-five was the passing score with a P or F posted on your cover sheet in the upper left hand corner. I couldn't imagine what General Gardner would do if anyone had failed. I assumed the failure would be quarantined and isolated until the mission was complete

Along with Prentice and Dawson, Boeing Vertol sent three additional staff pilots from their training department to act as our flight instructors for a period not to exceed 90 days.

After taking and passing all the ground school tests I had the remainder of Friday and the weekend to study the standard operating and emergency procedures on the H34. It was compulsory to be prepared to fly three two-hour flights every day for the next week with Friday set for the A13 check ride.

Examining the pages of my logbook I discovered I hadn't flown the H34 for nearly three years. Reasoning told me it was going to be an out-of-the-ordinary week.

From early Monday morning through late Thursday evening I finished in its entirety all of my flight training with the exception of the check-ride. Since our mission was to take place under the cover of darkness Command thought it was best to give the final check late at night. Everything went well and I was determined to be qualified on the UH34D as an Aircraft Commander. The Operations Clerk made an entry in my logbook signifying I was fully qualified in the UH34D as an Aircraft Commander. I couldn't have been in higher spirits.

Of the five pilots in Section 1 flying the prior Friday night each man passed. It would take an additional five weeks to complete the remaining pilots in Sections 1 and 2. In the meantime, those who had the A13 out of the way would begin preparations for carrier qualifications on the USS Valley Forge.

The steady grind of day and night flying, studying with little recreation was beginning to take its toll on the men. Of all the individuals I had expected to fail it certainly wasn't my roommate.

Returning to my room I discovered Glenn and all his possessions were gone. It was if he'd never been there. Wiped clean. One positive outcome from all the training and studying was that all Crew Chiefs and Gunners completed the standardized tests and check-rides without a single failure. That in itself spoke well for our enlisted personnel.

It was uncomfortable knowing Glenn had fallen short and had to face the consequence of his failure. Any calamity from A to Z would set him free of the obligation of flying in Operation At Morning's Light and its dangers. At Morning's Light had one pure unadulterated fact which is that Glenn was going to be quarantined here at Camp Pendleton until the Battle of Jericho had come to its final conclusion.

Who knows? Maybe he asked to be dropped from the program. Like the rest of us he knew nothing of this mission beforehand. Glenn probably was content with his assignment at his former duty station flying aircraft and knew he would be without the fear of war and the pain it brings to one and all. He certainly didn't choose to be in the compound with us. He certainly didn't volunteer.

Glenn's present contract with the Corps was about to expire and the probability of him receiving an extension for an additional three years of active duty was close to nil. As a consequence it was going to be a sad day for him and his family.

He was an outstanding Marine, yet the Corps wasn't asking me for a letter of recommendation or an endorsement of approval. The Corps never barters or gives anything other than the opportunity for an individual to advance in rank and to consent to duty without question.

It is always God, Country, Corps... in that order.

CHAPTER 16

CARRIER QUALIFACATIONS
RECON BRIEF CAPTAIN SCANLON

USS Valley Forge LPH8 off the coast of California

The two final phases of training that remained off record and listed as incomplete were carrier qualifications and Op Order 364. Our

goal was to make roughly 10 night landings or more and then close out with Op Order 364. The Op Order transferred all the pilots and crewmembers to the USS Valley Forge (LPH-8) for 7 days of training. First we were to get our 10 landings aboard ship. Everyone completed this in one evening. Completing the carrier qualifications, we were then briefed repeatedly on the planned and desired attack on Jericho. Every night for the following six days, with all hands onboard the Valley Forge, a full brief went down.

All the upper echelon, plus anyone and everyone of any importance involved on the attack on Camp Jericho would be in attendance. Command level personnel, airborne ops, recon/ rifle teams, representatives from the various ships in the task force, search and rescue, doctors, hospital corpsmen... You name it they were there. The Pilots Ready Room was too small to accommodate the personnel involved so the meeting was moved to the hanger deck. This area was secured from the rest of the ships personnel by our Marine Security Team. They constructed and provided, along with their Guard Dogs, an enclosure that prohibited unwanted intruders.

Personnel from the Fleet Marine Force, individuals from 2/5 (2nd Battalion/5th Marines) stationed at Camp Pendleton were commandeered as camp prisoners. To make our mission more genuine and convincing, Colonel Holiday incorporated simulated radio failures, as well as crashes and rescues, throughout the exercise. Flying off the Valley's deck in the dark of night, landing in simulated campgrounds and returning to the ship with our repatriated personnel for seven straight nights over a week had been exhausting. Colonel Holiday didn't anticipate what would happen on the final night of our training.

That night, we began closing out the evening, shuttling the Grunts of 2/5 off the ship and back to the staging area and their barracks at Camp Horno. After dropping off his last load of troops at Camp Horno, YK 14 and his crew were returning to the ship and had been cleared for a visual approach to spot 7. Fatigue must have been a factor as he lost control of the aircraft and crashed into the port side of the ship.

Falling into the water, it took just minutes before everyone on the flight deck and in the cat walks lost sight of her as she sunk below and into the deep dark blue water.

Immediately, search and rescue went into action. From the Bridge the Captain of the Valley Forge marked the latitude and longitude on the ship's charts where the accident occurred, launched the lifeboats and ordered those assigned to the Search and Rescue Aircraft to launch to the area where the aircraft had gone into the water.

We continued our search the entire evening and the remainder of the next day looking for survivors. After 48 Hours of searching and with little hope of rescue the search was called off. The crew and aircraft

were listed as missing at sea and presumed dead.

Search and Rescue units from Camp Pendleton, the Naval Air Station from San Diego and the U.S. Coast Guard continued the search for several days using radar to assist naval divers to recover the aircraft and the remains of the crew. All crewmembers were recovered and were to be buried with full military honors.

Following the termination of our search-and-rescue efforts the entire squadron met in the ship's Ready Room. Colonel Holiday spoke briefly of the unfortunate loss of our fellow shipmates and reminded us we must continue on with the mission at hand.

On the QT, he changed the status of a specific alternate pilot and crew to an active replacement. The standby crew had studied, trained and prepared themselves in chorus with us and instantaneously accepted their new position in the unit. General Gardner knew they would follow suit without any hesitation.

As the early morning sun emerged ever so slightly into the sky all hands were up and about or bright eyed and bushy tailed, ready to meet the day's challenges.

To start, the day officers and enlisted alike took care of the three S's (shit, shower and shave). After morning chow in their respective mess halls all personnel were directed to be in the Ready Room at 0900 hours without fail to receive a briefing from Captain Phillip Scanlon, the Commanding Officer Company A of the 3rd Reconnaissance

Battalion out of Camp Butler Okinawa, Japan. He and his team had all

the vital information needed to complete our mission.

With all men present, Colonel Holiday entered the ready room just before 0900 hours. Someone called out, "Attention on deck!" With that the entire room grew quiet. Only the sounds of men rising from their seats were heard. We stood at attention until Col. Holiday called out, "At ease. Take your seats."

The Colonel's opening statement was short and to the point. "On my left stands Captain Phillip Scanlon. He is here to tell you of the obstacles and dangers you will be facing at Jericho. Captain Scanlon, you have the floor."

Captain Scanlon had our undivided attention.

Watching him, I remember being amazed by his stature. Captain Scanlon was not a large man nor was he small. He was about 5' 8" in height, and he had dark brown hair and fair skin. He couldn't have weighed more than 165 pounds. He had just one ribbon over his left breast pocket, the Silver Star. There were no other ribbons indicating where he had been and why he had received such an award.

In a pre-briefing from the Colonel we knew Captain Scanlon grew up in Phoenix, and he had received his Bachelors of Science Degree from a small school called Almont University in Michigan. His degree and major were in Secondary Education and from what we could tell he wanted to teach biology at the high school level. A career change took place when his best friend was killed in Vietnam in 1968. After

learning of this tragic occurrence he applied for and was accepted into

the Marine Corps Officers Candidate School at Quantico, Virginia.

His enlistment into The Officers Candidate Program began one week after he graduated from college. Completing OCS his rise to the rank of Captain was swift. He was an excellent officer who attacked each of his assignments with serious-minded passion resulting in being promoted to the rank of Captain with minimum time in each of his former ranks of 2nd and 1st Lieutenants.

Completing OCS at Quantico, he was immediately transferred to Camp Lejeune near Jacksonville, North Carolina, for Advanced Infantry Training. With AIT completed, he received orders and was transferred to Camp Butler Okinawa, Japan. His application requesting to be assigned to the 3rd Reconnaissance Battalion had been evaluated and accepted with enthusiasm.

After passing through the gates of Camp Butler on the island of Okinawa he checked into Battalion headquarters and was immediately given command of Company A of the 3rd Battalion. His first assignment and orders came from The Joint Chiefs through Colonel A. J. Roberts the Battalion Commander of Special Operations. He admitted to being stunned about that one.

Scanlon was to assemble a Recon Team to be deployed on a top-secret mission into a country that was formally known as South Vietnam. He was to prepare and train a small group of men from Company A to enter, observe and plan an operation that would be used at a later date to accomplish the escape of known Prisoners of War. The North Vietnamese were holding and refusing to release these POWs after the Paris Peace Talks ended in March of 1973. The President wanted these

men returned and could care less if any country, kingdom, republic or other nation criticized our actions. We wanted all our POWs returned.

That meant any requests to The Chief of Naval Operations or The Commandant of the Marine Corps in the way of equipment or personnel would be granted, assembled and trained to fulfill our needs and requirements. The requests would be forwarded via Colonel A. J. Roberts Battalion Commander of Special Operations on the pre-briefed code.

Training was to be completed as soon as possible, because the Prisoners of War were U.S. officers, pilots and individuals that were privy to sensitive materials and specific persons that had knowledge of weapons systems our counterparts in Russia needed and wanted. They were being detained without their consent and the Joint Chiefs wanted them repatriated using the skills of Marine personnel trained in Black Operations. The Joint Chiefs feared that they were to be transferred within the next six months or sooner, which meant time was now of the essence.

What we heard that day came with the full approval of Brigadier General Paul Gardner Deputy, Commander U. S. Marine Forces Special Operations Command, Camp Pendleton. Everyone in the room sat perfectly still as we anxiously awaited Captain Scanlon's next words.

"In early June I assembled a small but effective team of five to infiltrate, conduct surveillance, identify and observe our intended target Camp Jericho, day and night," he announced. "I have prepared a battle plan that will overwhelm the troops stationed and

guarding the U.S. Servicemen at this specific campsite and free our known Prisoners of War. It was also my job to select the men I knew that would be able to complete the initial and opening phase of headquarters objectives."

It was at this point that he described and defined the men that assisted him in collecting the necessary information and facts Command would need to finalize and approve the preparations on Operation At Morning's Light.

"My reconnaissance unit made two entries and exits into Vietnam, and were discovered by North Vietnam soldiers and Vietnamese citizens both times. On each and every occasion that we were discovered, the enemy failed to live to tell anyone their story. They were silently and swiftly disposed of and obviously hidden somewhere in the jungle, never to be found again. They are probably listed at their command as AWOL while the citizens are reported to the local police as missing persons."

The Captain stared at us. "Here's the real shocker. At first I was stunned when I learned Company A of the 3rd Battalion was filled with liars, cheats, fighters, poker players, whoremongers, drunks, the worst of the worse, but the kind of men that possessed the characteristics I desired and wanted attached to my scout team."

He looked serious as hell. "I wanted Marines that were willing to give their lives for the red, white and blue and, if necessary, complete their journey in the Corps by being laid to rest in America's famous cemetery, Arlington National in Washington, D.C. They would be ready to salute their Commander in Chief in Heaven and firmly

believed that every Marine in Company A had spent their time in Hell here on earth and had earned a spot next to the Almighty upstairs."

He had the right group.

Scanlon told us Colonel Roberts had placed all the troublemakers, misfits and shit-birds that were constantly getting into trouble into Company A. The CO always assigned his newly arriving Captains to A Company. He wanted them to learn how to deal with degenerates without nearing or closing in on psychological collapse themselves.

Captain Scanlon continued. "The five men I have selected are the worst of the worst and, without a doubt, I have selected them because they were the nastiest and wickedest in the entire unit."

He looked around the room. "The rank and file of Company A is full of obedient, troubled assholes. They are to the man the foulest, evilest and cruelest battle-toughened individuals who will fight anyone, day or night. They will engage anyone of any size, any place and at a moment's notice. They are the meanest Marines in the Corps and that is why I want them on my team. They have one trait that is perpetual… and I promise you it will never be broken. It is their commitment to the Corps. Death before dishonor!"

CHAPTER 17

RUN WITH THE WIND

Captain Scanlon had to choose the best of men… the best of Marines… and during the interviewing process he realized what a challenge it might be. He told us that every man in the company had a "limited vocabulary." He knew they could use the words, "fuck," "fucker" and "fucking" in any given sentence, but that wouldn't deter him from looking at the men's credentials as Marines who fought bravely. It was obvious that the men had little regard for senior officers, though they did at least open their communications with "Sir."

After probing and reviewing the SRBs (Service Records Books) of the 150 men in his company Scanlon chose five of the most fearless and courageous men to lead the mission.

"Each and every one of the five endured two tours of duty in Vietnam, fighting mostly in the A Shau Valley and Quang Nam Province," Scanlon explained. "All have decorations for heroism and have been wounded at least twice, yet they continued unrepentant in battle under the nastiest of circumstances."

He continued. "As Marines they are the best. That means as a Marine

off duty, drunk or sober they are kinfolk to the pit bull looking to kick somebody's ass. Pass them on the street, give them a dirty look or say something out of the ordinary and you'd be burnt toast."

Here Scanlon paused to assess the room before continuing.

"They have been on report so many times for fighting it is unlikely they would even think of running out on you in a firefight. After a firefight or an engagement these men guarantee that there will be no survivors for the enemy to take home; just the dead. They do what needs to be done. I believe every Viet Cong or NVA Soldier they encountered would never again aim a rifle at one of their brother Marines."

Continuing with his brief, Scanlon said he had carefully chosen a Staff Sergeant, Jamie R. Stone. His home state was Montana, which at the time had a population of about 500,000. Stone was one of 20 Sioux Indians out of the total population and who had volunteered to serve in the Marine Corps during the Vietnam War.

He stood 5' 10", weighed about 190 pounds and was as ugly as sin. It must have been difficult for him to look in the mirror and see his reflection. He had scars just about everywhere on his face and body, a result of enduring several battles in the war. When completing the review of the reports in his military jacket Scanlon came to the conclusion that he was not only hard to look at but meaner than a junkyard dog. He was a Doberman through and through.

He went on to explain Sgt. Stone to us and eventually got around to why "Stony" was chosen. "His hair... black as coal. His face was

what one would expect looking into the eyes of a full-blooded Sioux Indian with high cheekbones, dark brown eyes and skin the color of bronze. It was obvious he carried the physical characteristics of his forefathers."

Scanlon kept talking. "Sgt. Stone or Stony as the men called him loved to fight and was always on the brink of being busted or discharged less than honorably. He didn't care. If he were to be discharged honorably or dishonorably he said his life style wouldn't change as he'd return to his lodge on the river and never be mistreated by the White Man ever again. Also noted in his Service Record Book was his Sioux name, Run With The Wind."

Apparently Stony failed to graduate from high school yet scored 115 on his incoming IQ test. Intelligent but lazy in regards to class work, but smart as a whip. Did well in all other incoming tests but requested to go infantry rather than to a demanding school that required effort and study.

Scanlon continued on by guiding us through Run With The Wind's background. "Sgt. Stone was born and raised on the banks of the Gallatin River, northwest of Bozeman, Montana, and that he was a member of the Oglala tribe, one of the seven tribes of the Lakota. Growing up as a Sioux Indian boy he became familiar with the ways and customs of his forefathers."

Scanlon said he'd discovered that Stone's specialty as a youngster was the bow and arrow and that he could hit a target dead center at 25 yards. "Somehow, someway," Scanlon said, "I knew I could use that extraordinary talent sometime during one of the two reconnaissance

inserts the Joint Chiefs of Staff had requested of me and my team. Silent death to someone might be needed to protect discovery."

Scanlon seemed a bit smitten with Stony as he continued telling us about the young man. He was obviously in awe of the young man's talents with the bow and arrow. "As a boy Sgt. Stone learned and was taught what Mother Earth meant to the Oglala's, which is the gift of life. He learned where the tribe's major battles with the Whites took place and had a constant desire to learn more and more. Throughout his youth, during the warm months of summer, Stony set out on his pony to explore the battlegrounds of his ancestors."

Scanlon waved his hand across the air as if he could almost see the scene.

"During his journeys he lived off the land. It was a breeze for Stony. As a young man his elders taught him how to trap animals for food and he was introduced to the plants that were suitable to eat and he was educated on those that would either poison a person or make him extremely ill.

"Identifying safe food was never a problem as the squaws taught him when he was a little boy what he should or shouldn't eat. There were wild cherries, strawberries, plumbs, gooseberries and currents that grew throughout the summer months that were effortlessly accessible to him as he traveled in search of his history.

"He followed the banks of the Yellowstone. He covered and walked the grounds around the Bighorn Rivers. He saw where Custer made his last stand. The Sweetwater and the North Platte Rivers gave him food as he made and studied his way through his past."

Scanlon told us he was mystified as he listened as Run With The Wind told him his stories, like how he would sit as close as he could without being discovered and listen to the elders talk about the days of the 1860s and 1870s as they sat in council around the campfire.

Names like Fort Reno, Fort Phil Kearny, Fort Smith, and all the forts along the Bozeman Trail were vividly brought to mind, because they were intense and graphic in their collective memory. There's something to be said of stories passed from generation to generation, Scanlon told us. "As the elders told stories of the great warriors of the past as they sat by the warmth of the fire, Stony told me it was as if he lived in that era and visualized his great-grandfather's strength and courage. He told me that listening to the elders speak of the old days he learned there were millions of buffalo that crossed their lands and that the Whites destroyed them by the hundreds for their skins. He discovered what the feather of the eagle meant as they went to battle and why they painted their pony before battle and what colors. His knowledge of the past was incredible!"

We were mesmerized by what Scanlon was saying. To say the least, the Marine he spoke of wasn't an ordinary, run-of-the-mill brave Marine. He was like a Super Marine. Scanlon said that many times Run With The Wind prayed to the gods and asked them why he hadn't come from Mother Earth at the time when Chief Red Cloud was leading his people. Those councils he listened to while the elders spoke around the circle of fire taught him the Oglala Warrior's side of the story. The book of lies written by the Blue Coats and Buffalo Soldiers filled him with resentment, pain and hatred.

Scanlon added, "Growing up with his Oglala bothers Run With The Wind learned about The Bozeman Trail that originated in Nebraska, moved northwest and ended at Virginia City. Scores of attacks along the trail against the gold seekers and wagon trains were many with men like John Bozeman, John Jacobs and Jim Bridger offering guide service guaranteeing safe passage yet were unable to provide protection from the so-called savages of the west."

Stony's interview with the Captain ended up being far more than a way for Captain Scanlon to get to know him; it became a lesson in history about the Sioux, as well as how campaigns that were won by the Whites were called "Victories" while victories by the Sioux were identified as "Savage Massacres."

The Bureau of Indian Affairs and the great White Chief Abraham Lincoln attempted to make treaties with the seven tribes of the Sioux; treaties the whites failed to keep with his people.

Sgt. Stone was Scanlon's first draft pick for the mission. In Scanlon's words, this Marine was a calloused, angry man at the age of 28 and Scanlon wanted him on the team. We found ourselves wanting him on the team, too.

CHAPTER 18

FILES/LOCKS/WILLS

S canlon's second and third picks were Privates First Class Ivan Files and Leon Locks. Both men were from the Bronx in New York City, had graduated at the bottom of their class from their local high school, were partners in crime since their early teenage years and committed a multitude of mandatory and compulsory crimes in order to become members of the neighborhood street gang called "The Storms."

These two men lived in poverty and made their homes in fatherless, run-down, rat-infested housing. They were survivors and could get through anything. Everything that was of any value to them they had stolen on the dirty streets of the Bronx, yet neither man had ever stolen from their fellow Marines.

According to Scanlon, by day these guys hung out on street corners harassing those in the area, and by night they were thieves, never missing an opportunity to rob from any passerby, including women and the elderly. They liked easy targets or those that wouldn't put up a fight to keep their possessions. They had little respect for anyone and their only goal and passion in life was to enter the street gang. They were recognized in the neighborhood as "Storm hopefuls," reflected by the blue bandanas they wore around their foreheads.

Both had been arrested for burglary and drug offenses; both plead guilty after a bargaining session with the District Attorney. As they stood before the District Judge of the Federal Court they were given a choice. Either join the United States Army or the U. S. Marine Corps, or go to jail for three to five years for burglary and an additional two years for possession of marijuana with the intent to sell.

The Public Defender representing Files and Locks recommended they make their decision without delay and accept the judge's recommendation. Scanlon told us, "Looking each other in the eye they nodded their heads in the affirmative and decided to go into the Marine Corps rather than being someone's bitch in the local penitentiary."

Scanlon went on to tell us that Ivan and Leon were African Americans that had lost interest in school early on and had very little knowledge of science, math or the arts. This was not because they lacked the intelligence to learn but rather because their concentrated efforts lead them down a different path.

Both Ivan and Leon were small in size, but they had proven their worth as they were defending Hill 880 North during the siege of Khe Sanh in 1968.

Additionally they had scouted and patrolled many trails of the Quang Tri Province in search of the enemy and were familiar with the area surrounding the DMZ where Camp Jericho was located. Their knowledge of the region and the ability to identify areas of safety would be invaluable to the group as a whole if and when it was ever

needed. They weren't the sharpest knives in the drawer, but these men knew the subject area well.

The fourth in the selection of men was a corporal who came from Kodiak, Alaska. He was born on the kitchen table without the help of a doctor or nurse and raised in a four-room log cabin with his mother, father and two brothers on Kodiak Island. His name was Gary Wills and was a true outdoorsman.

He was of above-average size and weight, and he had been home-schooled by his mom. His testing level was equal to the seventh grade, but his understanding of the outdoors and ability to live off the land under any weather conditions made him desirable to the group.

Scanlon told us that as a teenager about the age of 16 Wills was alone on a deer hunt when he stumbled upon the carcass of a freshly killed moose. Without warning, out of the bush charged a full-grown Grizzly running at full speed toward him. The scream of the animal was deafening as it got closer and closer. He had no choice but to drop to the ground, roll his body face down and wrap his hands and arms around his head.

Scanlon said that Wills told him during his interview that the attack was to the neck area at first and then the bear grabbed him by the thigh. Wills said that with her razor sharp teeth she ripped through his leg and shook him several times before tossing him at least eight feet from the carcass. Lying motionless for at least two minutes, but what to Wills seemed like a whole lot longer, the beast continued to savagely bite and rip at his torso and legs before finally deciding his victim would no longer bring harm to her cubs or steal her food.

Wills remained motionless for what seemed like an hour as the Grizzly finally covered its kill with leaves and disappeared from the area with her two cubs.

Struggling to get on his feet it never entered Will's mind to surrender the will to live. His continued concentration on living kept him going and alive. Eventually he made it to an area where he had seen campers earlier in the day.

Seeing him and learning of the attack the campers placed him in the back of their truck and raced him to the nearest hospital. Six weeks later Wills was well enough to be released from the hospital as an ambulatory discharge. He walked with a limp and gave God a thank you for the continuance of life.

Drafted into the Marine Corps Wills was transferred to Company A when they discovered he wasn't as bright as the average recruit. He repeatedly told the officers and men in his unit about his fight with the Grizzly, showed them his scars and picked up the nickname 'Grizzly.'

On occasion the men in the unit would call him "Stupid Grizzly." He must have rearranged the faces of at least six Marines for calling him stupid. All required trips to sick bay and a visit to the doctor for stitching and bandaging. Calling Grizzly stupid made him livid to which he responded in violence. After being on the receiving end of Grizzly's wrath, the other Marines ceased the use of the word "stupid" in reference to Grizzly.

As we sat there we anticipated and figured it out that the fifth man on the team was none other than Captain Scanlon himself. "Speaking as the leader of the team, the fifth and final man in the group is … me. If anything happens to me while we are on patrol, Run With The Wind or Sergeant Stone will take over as leader. Any Questions?"

There were none and the unit broke for lunch.

CHAPTER 19

TEAM CAPTURED FIRST ENTRY/ESCAPED

Af. ter lunch the unit returned to training building at 1300 hours for a continuance of Captain Scanlon briefing.

"With the training of my men completed at Camp Hanson, Okinawa, our team was ordered aboard the USS Bluegill a WWII submarine that would transport us to a position off the coast of Vietnam designated RED HOT. "

The USS Blue Gill leaving the Naval Base Naha Okinawa, Japan

"The Bluegill is the only ship in the United States Navy to be named after a freshwater sunfish that swims in the waters of the Mississippi River Basin and most of the fresh water lakes in the northeastern states. She was a Gato-Class diesel-electric sub with a crew of 60 men; six officers with 54 enlisted. She has six forward and four aft torpedo tubes, one 50-caliber deck gun and one 20mm cannon on her forward deck."

Continuing with his brief Scanlon told us, "My men boarded the Sub and within 30 minutes two of them had been involved in a fight with four sailors. The Navy gave the Marines the best they had to offer... for about three minutes."

Two had severe cuts on their faces requiring stitches, one had a broken arm and one was down for the count. Needless to say, the Captain of the ship was a bit on the angry side and consequently restricted the entire unit in the forward torpedo room for the duration of the cruise.

Scanlon added, "The ship's Captain told us that he couldn't wait to get us to our destination and off his ship."

Scanlon went on to add that he was a smart mouth back then and responded with, "Likewise, Captain! We're not squid and prefer being on Terra Firma, Sir. Treat my men like the men they are or I can get your ass into a whole lot of trouble. If you doubt my word just try me... Sir."

This brought a wave of low laughter to the room.

Scanlon continued briefing us about the mission. "The bluegill is able to stay on patrol for 75 days and submerged for 48 hours. The plan was to arrive at Red Hot at 2400Z when the night was the darkest (moonless) and would leave the Marines time enough to paddle to shore, hide their equipment in the bush, saddle up and start their trip inland still under the cover of darkness."

He said that about two miles off the beach, the Captain of the Bluegill placed two black rubber rafts over the side. One raft for Scanlon's team and the other for all the equipment that would be required or needed to complete the mission --radios, cameras, weapons, ammunition and food.

After the completion of their mission they were to rendezvous with the Bluegill at 0300 hours at Red Hot in seven days' time for their extraction. The Captain, still angry over the severe beating his men took prior to their departure, made it clear to Caption Scanlon and his tough guys, "There will not be a second effort to retrieve your team. If they were a no show they would be written off as MIA."

Scanlon said he replied, "Captain, you remember what I said. If need be, I can have you swabbing decks in a Mess Hall. Trust me; it's the truth. If you leave us behind you'll be sorry."

Scanlon went on by telling us his unit was to establish an inbound route as well as detailing maps for exiting the camp.

"When my recon team reached shore we called feet dry and moved inland. Receiving that call, the Bluegill disappeared into the depths of the China Sea. Dawn was breaking with the sun just coming up on

the eastern shore when two NVA Soldiers discovered and captured us. However, it was strictly by accident. We were so involved hiding escape equipment and charting it on a map that we dropped our guard and were overtaken with little struggle or contest."

Scanlon told us he always had Run With The Wind with his bow and arrow at the ready as a trailer lagging behind by about ten yards or so. He called it his "quiet death option and last resort opportunity for escape." In this instance, it would prove to be an excellent plan.

The senior NVA soldier had taken weapons from Scanlon and his men, made them lie face down with their hands behind their backs and directed his partner to tie them up. While he held his weapon on Scanlon's team and the other was tying them up, their attention was solely on their captives.

With the first NVA Soldier standing behind and to the left of his subordinate he was open for a clean shot from Run With The Wind. The first Sioux arrow struck mid chest of one of the NVA Soldiers. He silently and immediately fell to his knees, grabbing at his chest. His partner never knew what happened. He never would. Run With The Wind's second arrow stuck the man in the neck, and the short contest was over. Scanlon's team may have been detected, but the NVA Soldiers would never live to tell anyone their story.

"Gathering our wits about us we knew we had to be more on guard in moving forward," said Scanlon. "Making our way westward toward our destination our progress was more and more tiring. What energy we had was drained from us as night became day. We knew that June was Vietnam's summertime with the average daytime temperature ranging between 71 and 78 degrees. We had prepared for the heat and humidity while training in Okinawa, but the heat in this tropical forest made our movement backbreaking work. It was beginning to wear us down with all the equipment we carried."

He added, "Beyond the heat and humidity we faced were the Anamosa Cordillera Mountains. They ran parallel to the coast, stood in front of us and rose in some places to over 6000 feet. Forest cover and grasses had declined 50 percent due to the war with U.S. Forces spraying approximately 65 million gallons of herbicides, including Agent Orange. We noticed that some foliage was beginning to recover as we made our way toward Camp Jericho."

Scanlon took a breath before continuing with his briefing.

"It took my team roughly 72 hours from the Bluegill to Camp Jericho. On the way I ordered some of my men to take short naps while others stood watch in the surrounding bush. (Two hours on; two hours off)`. We could have made our destination sooner but would have been exhausted with little reserve energy remaining.

"Our biggest problem was the mountain ranges. Rather than going direct by climbing, we circumvented them by going around the foothills and following a riverbed until we were safely on other side and into the valley. It took us virtually three days to finally arrive at Camp Jericho. We rested and slept only during the heat of the day.

"After their arrival at Jericho we observed, photographed and counted enemy personnel, we drew plans of the site and monitored all their activities. We had it down to the minute when it came to

their routine throughout the day and evening. Little did they know, but we would be back later to recover those that they thought we left behind."

Then the briefing took a turn. Scanlon went into detail about how his men had been discovered and what transpired right before Run With The Wind put an arrow in each of the captors.

"Remember how I said my men were taken accidentally? Well, on 12 June two of my men were discovered by NVA Soldiers who lived in a nearby village," said Scanlon. "After my men were taken captive, one of the NVA Soldiers who spoke English asked what they were doing with all the medicine, ammunitions and weapons. My men told them they found all this stuff along the trail and that they were deciding what to do with all their newly found treasures. They told the enemy that they were deserters from the war and asked not to be given them back to the Americans. The captured men gave up without a fight and started begging for their lives."

The room was hushed. We didn't know what Scanlon would say next, but the way he told the story was mesmerizing.

Scanlon said, "What the NVA Soldiers didn't know was that there were three of the remaining members of our team in the surrounding area just waiting for the right moment to respond and take action to save their teammates. One of the team in the bush on guard was Run With The Wind who had drawn his bow and arrow and waiting for just the right moment. On my order both North Vietnamese soldiers had a silent arrow in their bodies within seconds of each other. The

first shot was driven into the heart and the other entering the temple area and out the lower part of his skull."

Scanlon added, "Since the NVA Soldiers would never be heard from again, their unit would probably have placed them on the desertion list. We disposed of the men's bodies humanely and quietly. They died for their country; we lived for ours."

At this point, with story time over, Sgt. Rockwell, a member of the second and larger recon unit that would be inserted with team one to begin the operation, started handing out the amended overlays and our battle plans. We were to read and memorize the details, keep overlays for our charts and destroy all remaining documents.

He told us, "We'll be waiting for your choppers at Camp Jericho 75 hours after our initial call… 'Up and Happy.' My team and 36 former captives will be waiting for transportation to Libertyville."

CHAPTER 20

TO THE WEST AND THE PACIFIC

We were no longer members of Section 1 or Section 2. We were a rock-solid unit that now is one for all, all for one. With Scanlon's briefing about his experiences in the area where we were headed… his way of warning us of how to behave… we were moving forward on a mission that The Joint Chiefs, The Special Operations Command and The Commandant of the Marine Corps had organized and ordered operational.

Our unit was optimistically hopeful that Operation At Morning's Light would be successfully drawn to a conclusion with a minimum of misfortune or causalities. All of us were in agreement as to what had to be done, the methods we needed to undertake and the promise we made to one another: Bring Our Brothers Home.

CC wanted us to have a few days' free time but it was not to be. Much to our surprise, at morning muster we discovered it was moving day. We were told to label and pack everything we owned in newly issued military duffle bags, tag them with our name, throw them on the trucks parked just outside the compound and climb aboard military buses located in the same lot. Departure time would be 0930 hours.

Anticipation filled the campgrounds. This was what we had trained for, and now it was time for all of us to bring it into being.

These vehicles would take us approximately 30 miles north on highway 5 to Marine Corps Air Station El Toro in California. At El Toro two C130 aircraft would be waiting on the tarmac at Base Operations to transport us to MCAS Futenma, Okinawa, via Anchorage, Alaska, and to Iwakuni, Japan. We were not to discuss our mission with any of the C130 flight crews and to reply by saying we were being transferred to the Far East as reserves to various units on Okinawa.

Another surprise is that we were broken down into Section 1 and Section 2 once again. That way, if anything tragic happened to one of the Sections we could continue with our mission using the remaining crews and aircraft. Section1 C130A Section 2 C130B.

Flight deck of C130

C130 0n the tarmac at El Toro/ and flight deck

By the time we made our landing on Okinawa we discovered the U.S.S. Princeton was still working its way to Naha, Okinawa, from the U. S. Naval Base Yokosuka, Japan, and the U.S.S Webster was still coming from San Diego with our birds. With the Webster and the Princeton still at sea we were without any quarters to call our own and no aircraft to complete our mission.

There we were on the tarmac at Marine Corps Air Station Futenma, exhausted, with everything we owned in a duffle bag and no place to stow our gear. Two hours later General Gardner passed the word he had found us temporary quarters while waiting for the Princeton to arrive.

The offensive and malicious dialogue started when we learned we were to be garrisoned in an abandoned hanger located at the south end of the airfield. Folding cots placed in rows within the hanger was the norm and that is what we would use until our ship made port.

French Barracks, 1964

The minute I saw the cots my memory flashed back to the old French Barracks we had for quarters in Da Nang, Vietnam. At that time we had four pilots to a room and all used a community shower and head.

This was the first time I had heard hard-core bitching from the group and I can hardly blame them. Our food source were C Rations that had dates stamped on the sides of the boxes as early as 1950. I know they're not supposed to go bad, but this was something else. Something nasty and somewhat insulting. Where was the treatment we had received during training?

I remembered eating rations like this while in Vietnam. Ham and lima beans were horrible. The troops called them "Garbage Cans"

and they couldn't give them away to the local population. The peanut butter had so such oil the only time we would eat it was when we had dysentery, because it was a temporary cure for the condition while in the field. Guys used to pour the oil off the top and use it as fuel for cooking. Crackers and jelly were okay, but it was hard to put down.

Interrupting my grumbling thoughts, General Gardner ordered lights out at 2200 hours and passed along to the troops in the strongest of Marine vocabulary with additional orders given not to leave the premises.

"Anyone leaving the hanger for any reason other than to piss or take a crap in the blue shitters outside door #3 will be arrested and dealt with later!"

SECURITY was the name of the game. There were a few "fuck yous" heard in the background, but the General let it pass. He was as exhausted as we were. Besides that, the sermons and lectures were over. It was time to rest, gather our thoughts, and study the battle plan and the codes used on the mission and their purposes.

After a day's wait spent killing time reading books, the Princeton and the USS Webster finally arrived in port and the transferring of our aircraft had already begun.

With the transfer in process we made our move to the Princeton and our final quarters. All of the officers and men were anxious to get to our assigned rooms and maybe even get in a few hours of rest on a real mattress. The cots were not the best; our backs ached and we didn't get a good rest on those damned cots.

My assigned room located in the Bow of the ship was about 8 feet by six feet with just enough room for a bunk bed and a desk. The desk had a tiny folding chair attached to a rail on the right side under the desktop. The user could pull it out from under the desktop anytime he had the need to sit at the desk while writing letters or filling out after-action reports. The room also had a safe mounted on the

bulkhead above the desktop. The closet barely had enough room to hold my uniform.

Everything from hatches and passageways to rooms and chairs, anything that was aboard that ship was painted Battleship Gray. Community showers were down the passageway. It was going to be close quarters for all.

After getting settled in our assigned rooms, word was passed that we were to muster at 0800 hours the following morning in the Pilot Ready Room for a briefing on Operation At Morning's Light. By 0835 hours we learned the size and what ships were in Task Force 34.21. It was no longer just an Op Order on paper; it was now assembled and readied at the U.S. Naval Base Naha in Okinawa, Japan.

TASK FORCE 34.21

1. USS Bluegill, SSK 242 submarine: served in WWll. Sunk 46,212 tons of Japanese shipping and one Japanese cruiser. Vietnam Era, Patrolled Gulf of Tonkin, reconnaissance and Pilot rescue. Primary purpose: to carry and insert Recon and Rifle teams 72 hours prior to the launching of all U.S. H34s.

2. One battleship/defensive and offensive purposes. USS New Jersey

3. USS Princeton LPH-5 (Landing Platform Helicopter 5).

4. USS Ranger, ship's complement: three squadrons of F4s, two squadrons of A4s, One squadron of Ads and one squadron A6s.

USS New Jersey

LPH5 USS Princeton

Men getting their carrier qualifications records completed

USS Princeton underway with operations in motion

USS Ranger with medic stations

5. Aircraft Control Center on Station: two airborne surveillance aircraft with radar controllers located to the Northeast and southeast of Jericho. Will arrive on station and be in position at Up and Happy + 70 hours.

Their primary and critical duty was to pass tactical information and assign targets to our fighters and attack aircraft once the operation begins. The Flagship and Combat Information Center (CIC) had overall command authority and was aboard the Battleship USS New Jersey.

After chow and with all hands in the Pilots Ready Room by 0800 hours we discovered that Tuna, (code name for the submarine in our Task Force) had pre-boarded four 6 man recon teams, four snipers for a total of 28 men from the 3rd Reconnaissance Battalion out of Camp Butler, and was already underway. They were to proceed and arrive at Red Hot with the USS Princeton arriving at the same position 72 hours later. The Blue Gill would disembark the 28 Marine Strike Force at Red Hot minus 72 hours.

Leaving Naha they were to run silent and run deep, cruising north of the Philippines, south of Taiwan, and slip into the South China Sea undetected and adjacent to the Paracel Islands. We were already on the clock.

Receiving word that Tuna had arrived at Red Hot and were in the process of disembarking the vanguard to the shoreline, they radioed the code words "Up and Happy," meaning our men had hit the beach undetected and were making their way inland. Pushing it hard, it would take 65 hours or less for the teams to cut through the jungle and around The Anamosa Cordillera Mountains to arrive at Jericho at 2100 HRS. The attack would begin at 0300, after observing the encampment, making sure their habits were true to character.

Their orders once on the ground and under way they were to "avoid contact with the enemy at all cost. Release of any persons captured whether it was civilian or military is not an option. Do what needs to be done without hesitation so as not to compromise the mission."

Both airborne surveillance aircraft were in standby mode on the tarmac at Paya Lebar Air Base in Singapore Island off the southern tip of the Malaysian Peninsula. They were given a departure time by CIC so as to arrive 100 nautical miles northeast of Red Hot at + 72 hours Up and Happy. Total distance they had to travel was approximately 918 Nautical Miles. Their aircraft had a range of 4600nm at a cruising speed of 290 knots.

Having all this information, the Princeton in the dark of night pulled out of port at precisely 0200 hours. This would put the 3rd Recon Battalion, Task Force 34.21 and Airborne Command simultaneously in position in precisely 72 hours. At that time the opening phase of Operation At Morning's Light would begin.

On this night, the weather forecast was calm seas with light and variable wind bearing little consequence. Most important, the moon was not in the night sky. This meant it would be extremely dark, giving our recon team a distinct advantage. While our sniper teams made their way to their objective or the kill point it would be very difficult for anyone, including the guards at Jericho, to pick up any movement in the bush.

The enemy on this Thursday evening was like all the other Thursday evenings our Marines had ever observed. They calculated and anticipated having on watch in the camp a grand total of 12 men, four of whom were positioned in towers at the corners of the encampment. Four additional men were walking the fences with four others sitting around a lighted table just outside their living quarters playing cards... just like during our practice runs.

It was anticipated that the men walking the fence and those that were at the table would leave their stations at around 2200 hours to gather up the prisoners and march them into a building that was assumed to be their lockdown quarters for the evening. As usual, the four at the table would relieve those in the towers for an eight-hour watch to be relieved at 0600 hours. At that time they would repeat the same routine just like each and every day. The four NVA Soldiers at the four corners were the only sentinels left on duty till 0600 hours and would be the first to die.

With the lockdown complete, the NVA that were relieved at the corner post entered a building that was assumed to be their regular living quarters. One of the eight always went to the radio shack and checked in with whomever was his superior officer and then returned to the building with the others of his detachment. All eight remained there throughout the night.

On one occasion, and only one, ladies of the night came to the main gate. Entering the compound, they remained with the guards for most of the evening before departing around 0430.

Our H34s were to wait for Recons arrival time of 2100HRs, then from 2100Hrs until 0300HRs they were to observe and monitor the activites of Jericho's prison gaurds to confirm the enemy was duplicating their daily habits. At 0300 if all behaviors of the encampment were authenticated and only four corner gaurds at their posts. The remainer of the guards were in their quarters in a deep sleep. Most likely their last. The code words "Trade Show Opened" could now be sent to CIC.

CHAPTER 21

LETTERS HOME/OPS BEGIN
CREW ASSIGNMENTS

With the mission to begin within the hour I made it a point to write a letter to my wife and my son. After sealing the letter to my wife and addressing the envelope, I didn't have time to finish my letter to Kirk. I would do it when I returned. Tension started to build within me as I thought about what was about to happen in the next 60 minutes.

Out of the past came one of the more perilous missions that refused to disappear from my memory. Sitting alone at my desk, sweat began to spread across my forehead. My right hand began to tremble. This always happened when I remembered a tragic event that came during my time in Vietnam. I felt an unsettling in my stomach and had the impulse to throw up. Would I ever forget?

It was the same thing over and over. A RPG had hit my aircraft in the tail section. Spinning around uncontrollably I desperately attempted every trick I knew to control the aircraft as it fell from the sky, impacting the ground just feet from those that wanted to kill me. In all the confusion I was still able to draw my side arm to fight off two NVA soldiers that had an unforgettable and very determined look in their eyes. It was a look that gave me an awareness of my impending death.

On this day the Lord had other plans. It wasn't my time to die.

Several Marines from the site I had just resupplied came to my rescue. I owe them my life and to this day their names and where they live are etched in my memory forever. Clearing my mind, my thoughts next went to my crew.

Being designated the Aircraft Commander on this mission, I was assigned aircraft YK22 along with its Crew Chief, Staff Sgt. Charlie Woodruff. He had been in the Corps for about 12 years with a record void of blemishes. He was formally a member of one of the most decorated helicopter squadrons in the Marine Corps, HMM 562, a.k.a., the Red Foxes.

The myth or mystique of why they were called the Red foxes was that they had shed more blood in total and awarded more Purple Hearts than any other squadron in the Corps. Sgt. Woodruff, whom I always called Woody, had three Purple hearts.

Woody stood about six feet tall, was built like the incredible Hulk and had a scar that ran across his forehead, left to right, down his disfigured eyelid and continuing down the right cheek. He was scary to look at. Proud of his scars, Woody displayed them as if they were battle ribbons on his dress uniform. He loved the look on the faces of people who met him for the first time.

The man grew up in a tiny town of Paducah, Kentucky, which had a general store, a service station, a post office and a single school. The grades kindergarten through the 12th grade had in its entirety about 150 students all taught in one large building.

Woody told me that every male living there in 1861 over the age of 16 had fought for the Confederacy during the Civil War. He always said that in his hometown they had fast horses, beautiful women and fighting forefathers who enjoyed killing Yankees. He neglected to remember the Civil War was over in 1865, yet it was always fun to see his fighting spirit. I guess that's why he hated the NVA. As he saw it, they were from North Vietnam and just another damned Yankee.

My co-pilot was a Captain Bobby Barnes. He received his orders to our group while flying in a squadron called the Evil Eyes based out of Tustin, California. In his SRB the rewards section showed he had received two DFCs for heroism in Vietnam. His combat record also revealed he was shot down twice around Hill 881 Northwest of Khe Sanh during Tet the NVA's massive offensive in 1968. He escaped capture both times. He had one Purple Heart and walked with a slight limp. His attitude was always positive. He was up for promotion to Major and welcomed an operation like this on his record.

Bruce Hatfield, my straphanger or gunner, had the appearance of being the youngest member in the entire unit. Baby faced, Hatfield didn't shave and all of us on the team thought maybe he lied about his age to get into the Corps.

He was a Marine, small in stature, slight of build and very, very quiet, but he held the rank of Sgt. He looked as if he should be a private. His squadron mates didn't know this guy was a real HERO... in capital letters. He had the Silver Star, a Bronze Star with Combat V and the Navy Cross for some incredible rescues he made after being wounded during several medical evacuations while flying as a crewmember in

the Quang Ngai Province. I called him Little Bad Bruce, like from the song "Big Bad Bruce."

Leaving my quarters I made my way to the supply room where the rest of the pilots were signing for and collecting the survival gear and weapons needed for this flight. Topside on the flight deck the crew chiefs were making last-minute systems checks on the aircraft: hydraulics, fuel, radios, navigation equipment and survival gear. Everything would be checked and rechecked, over and over again. At exactly 0300 hours, with all teams in position, the opening attack on Jericho began. With it a radio call was made to Rat Trap using the code words "Trade Show Opened."

Captain Phillip Scanlon and four of his team were in perfect position to take out the four tower guards all at one time. With scopes to their eyes, the four snipers with fingers on their triggers started a countdown. Each Marine had a handheld plunger attached to his rifle that when held in the down position sent a signal to and provided a green light on a tiny screen held by Captain Scanlon.

Each green light indicated that the tower guard was in a sniper's crosshairs and ready to kill.

With four tiny green lights showing on his screen, Captain Scanlon ordered, "Execute."

The four tower guards had less than a second to live. Four shots; four kills.

Following those first four shots, Operation At Morning's Light Marines' attack on hostile ground forces went swift and fatal. Back Pack (code name for Recon) sent and Home Plate received the following message: "Jericho in Shambles. One moaner, 1 bottom feeder, 21 Roadrunners, 27 walkers, total package costs half-dollar. Baby sleeping, awaiting tour bus."

Translated, the message read: "One Wounded in Action, one Enemy Prisoner of War and 21 Escapees. 50 seats needed. Everything under control. Quiet. Awaiting Greyhound for ride home."

Receiving that message, the Ops Officer on the Princeton cleared seven H34s for takeoff that had been on the flight deck engines and rotors engaged waiting for instructions. Beginning from spots 1 through 7, each aircraft received clearance for takeoff with the same departure instructions.

"Spots 1 through 7 cleared for takeoff in order, turn left heading three zero zero, climb to maintain 4000, contact Rat Trap button 2 (245.78 UHF)."

I was number 6 in order for lift off. Twenty tension-filled miles and 14 minutes later I would be there.

With our helos on their way, radar aboard one of the destroyers made contact with three Blue Bandits 300 degrees 50 miles high speed with a direct heading to Jericho. Rat Trap (airborne CIC) gave two F4s an intercept heading, altitude and distance.

"Shotgun, Roger Rabbit, targets at 270 degrees 35 miles 15 thousand."

Pressing on, Shotgun, the lead aircraft, armed his weapon systems, but he had to wait until they were inside 15 miles before firing his sidewinders. Locked on, he fired.

One of the approaching Migs flew right into the path of the approaching missile and exploded, immediately falling to the ground. The second aircraft disintegrated seconds later. The third a/c turned and ran before Shotgun could get a lock on.

Two aircraft down within minutes and one bugging out, all under the umbrella of secrecy. Only the After-Action Report (AAR) would tell the truth as it was Top Secret and wouldn't see the light of day for years to come.

Suddenly, Red Crown, our lone Battleship and primary CIC (Combat Information Center), called four Blue Bandits out of the southwest heading northeasterly toward Jericho. Ops immediately launched two additional F4s from the Ranger and gave four aircraft already airborne, intercept headings to the southwest.

Pressing on, our seven helos were getting closer to Jericho as we tried to make contact with Back Pack, our ground troops.

"Back Pack, this is Raptor. Do you read?"

Silence was the only response.

"Back Pack, this is Raptor. Do you read?"

Finally, loud and clear, we heard, "Raptor. LZ is cold. I repeat. LZ is cold."

Looking into the distance we saw that the recon guys had lighted the zones just like we practiced back at Pendleton so many times before this night. The only difference is that we were listening to all the radio calls about enemy aircraft pressing forward toward Jericho. So far, our Marine Brothers in their F4s were watching over us, making their intercepts and chalking up their kills.

Things were happening so quickly that it was hard to keep up with what was going on around us. Too much chatter on the radios. Our flight leader ordered everyone into trail. One behind the other, we followed his orders. Chatter on the radio got more intense as the Migs from the southwest grew closer.

Suddenly, our number-two man in EM 6 was hit by an RPG. His aircraft burst into flames and fell out of position. I watched in horror, as the aircraft broke apart as it spiraled to the ground. I wondered how anyone would survive that strike. The impact with the ground was frightening to witness.

Recon passed the word that they had 12 men on the move toward the crash site to see if there were any survivors.

As Marines that had fought in Vietnam in the past, again we had watched someone's brother, someone's husband or someone's best friend lose his life in the chopper that had crashed moments earlier. We knew the ropes. All of us had seen it before.

Our mission called for us to press on, disregard what had just occurred and get the package we came to rescue. We were Marines. We would do as ordered.

Waiting in the LZ after touchdown for the POWs to climb aboard brought back painful memories. It wasn't the first time I was a sitting duck, possibly in the crosshairs of an enemy rifle as I prayed he would miss his target.

I called out to Woody over the intercom, "Get 'em aboard! Hurry, Woody, get 'em on." Time crept by as if things were moving in slow motion.

After what seemed an eternity, I heard, "All hands aboard, Captain. Good to go." Welcome words…

Pulling up on the collective, our bird began to lift off when enemy fire began to strike the aircraft just about everywhere from front to rear.

All the fire came from our left.

Over and over we could hear the rounds striking the aircraft as I called out on the radio, "Taking fire from my left."

In seconds, an A4 was strafing and dropping napalm to my left as we started our departure. More and more rounds began to hit their mark. Where were they coming from? The LZ was supposed to be cold. Both crewmembers were retuning fire when Little Bruce, our straphanger, was hit and fell to the floor of the cabin.

Countless rounds struck the instrument panel as we gained speed in the initial climb. In quick time it was dark in the cockpit and I was flying by the seat of my pants. When Barnes tried to call me on the intercom it was inop.

He screamed as loud as he could, "I'm hit."

I asked him where and he responded, "Under the arm."

I yelled back, "Don't worry. We'll be home in twenty minutes!"

Our A4 pilots had been briefed to attack and destroy all vehicles northbound and southbound that appeared to be coming to the aid of Jericho. Somehow they missed a good number of trucks coming northbound with scores of NVA Soldiers onboard. In the planning stages this exact event had been anticipated and placed into the equation by S1 (Intelligence). We now hoped the NVA would jump from the trucks, run up the paths leading to the camp and step on mines placed by our troops on their first insert mission. It wasn't long before the contingency plan was doing the job it was intended to do.

I picked up what I thought was a good heading back to the Princeton. I was alone; solo with no escort or wingman and with an engine that was now running rough. Time remaining was now beginning to be my enemy. How long would it take me to find the ship? Would I make it back before the engine quit? Every minute that passed the damage and stress was taking its toll on my aircrafts engine as well as myself. Relief only came when I saw my ship off in the distance.

I pulled from the shoulder of my flight vest a small flashlight we always carried in the event we went into the water. I looked over all the instruments; everything appeared normal except the engine RPM. The engine oil was slowly draining away. Hydraulic fluids were still at the full levels. Holding the small light in my mouth, my scan included the three most important instruments: air speed, altitude and engine RPM.

The RPM surged up and down from 2700-2800 rpm occasionally to 3000, which was completely out of the normal range. It was considered an over-speed requiring an engine change. Like I really cared at this point. Just keep running till we get home EM 22… that's all I want. Just a few more minutes.

I called the ship and knew it was impossible to know if the Ops Officer or CIC heard me. I had to call in the dark. "Two wounded; excessive damage to aircraft. Engine running rough. Instrument panel inop. Cockpit in the dark. Need medical assistance. On straight in for spot 4."

I flipped the switches of my landing lights from on to off in an attempt to tell them my radio was inop. Only one light was functional. I kept talking to my aircraft. "Come on, Sweetheart, take me home. Just a few more miles. Make me a believer."

Paralleling the ship's course and holding the ship on my right I began slowing the airspeed as I approached the spot at a 45-degree angle. In no time I was over the deck, lower the collective, and set her down. I cut the mixture on the engine and engaged the rotor brake. Suddenly

there were people crawling all over the aircraft, aiding the wounded and taking them to sick bay.

Later they told me Little Bad Bruce had been killed outright and Captain Barnes succumbed shortly after arriving at hospital quarters. I received a quick physical check from the squadron's flight surgeon and was considered fit for duty. Doc Roswell sent me to the ready room for further assignment.

CC briefed me as to what had occurred in my absence and immediately reassigned me to another aircraft. This time it was search and rescue. At least 20 percent of the crews were either wounded or killed in the operation so far. I was told to relieve Lt. Archer in Rescue 2 as the Aircraft Commander.

I would be joining up with CC, the Aircraft Commander, on SAR One and we would be returning to the Jericho area.

CHAPTER 22

RESCUES ONE AND TWO

Forty-five minutes later Rescue 2 and my new crew from EM 14 were headed back into harm's way. I was with a crew I had never flown with before. I asked if Lt. Archer had briefed them. He nodded and said yes. Then I filled them in on what was going on at Jericho before we left the area. I called the mission and any like it a "Shit Sandwich," nothing less, nothing more.

After takeoff we picked up a compass heading of 235 and contacted CIC while climbing to four thousand feet. Red Crown gave us a quick briefing that an A4 that had been shot down with the pilot ejecting. He was unhurt but on the run. Not by choice but by circumstance he had to make his way out to the southeast following Escape Route 2.

The pilot's call sign was "Willie Willie." He had an AN/PRC 90 radio and specific questions to answer before a pickup would be made. CIC gave all the pilots questions in code and a new heading to the latest coordinates on Escape Route 2 that the pilot had just called in. He was about six miles away.

Transmitting on his PRC 90 Willie Willie responded that he was approaching X river on our maps with a clearing on the north side that a H34 could fit into easily.

Listing on the radio CC began asking the questions all rescue crews were required to ask of the pilot before a pick up would be attempted or made. The answers had to be correct since only the pilot would know the personal answers to all the questions. These same questions were on our kneepads written in an unusual code that we studied and learned at Pendleton while in classroom studies. The info was on all the pilots assigned to this particular mission.

CC began asking the pilot his series of questions and answers. "What's your wife's favorite color?"

"Red."

"Correct. What kind of dog do you own?"

"Poodle."

"Correct. What's his name?"

"Daisy, and she's a girl dog… not a male."

CC had tried to trick him, but all answers were positive, so we were good to go for the extraction.

"Willie Willie, when you hear the sound of us approaching pop a yellow smoke or a red smoke if zone is hot. When we get a visual we'll pick you up ASAP. Do You Read?"

Answering quickly, he said, "Hearing your approach, I will pop either a yellow smoke or a red depending on zone condition."

CC's aircraft while inbound for the pickup suddenly turned into a real can of worms. His engine failed and he auto rotated onto the bank of a nearby shallow riverbed. Without delay the downed pilot ran to the scene of the crash and began checking crew for injuries. Without delay I was on my approach in an attempt to pick up the entire group of airmen.

After landing, the gunfire seemed to come from everywhere. Suddenly two A4s came screaming by dropping and firing everything in their arsenal. The downed A4 pilot had contacted his brother Angels from above his position and relayed to them they needed ground support for the SAR crews. The noise was deafening but welcome.

Both my Straphanger and Crew Chief were returning fire with their weapons on full automatic. As CC, his Crewmembers and the downed pilot jumped into the belly of my aircraft the NVA concentrated all their firepower on the cockpit area. I couldn't get my ass outta there quick enough. The hits were too numerous to count.

Climbing to altitude I asked the Crew Chief if anyone needed medical assistance.

He said, "No, but the A4 pilot wanted to be dropped off on his ship so he could get back into the fight."

I responded with, "Tell him he's already cost his squadron an aircraft and about $850,000, so he's finished for the night. Get his name, rank and squadron. Tell him we want 100 bucks for the pickup and 50 bucks for every hit we took, and then we'll give him a ride back to the

Ranger. Maybe. For now he's going to the Princeton."

Speaking to the Crew Chief over the intercom I told him to lend the Exec his helmet and headset for a few seconds. I briefly spoke with CC, asking if he and his crew were okay.

His response was, "Thanks to you, we're all safe. No one is injured and I'm going to write you and every one of your crewmembers up for a citation or award when we get back to the ship. Your crew landed in the middle of a hornet's nest with complete disregard for your safety, and brought a full helicopter crew and an A4 pilot home on the same extraction. Well done, Marine, well done."

"Major, we were at the right place at the wrong time."

CC said, "From the bottom of my heart and from the rest of the men here in this cabin, we thank you! Thank you, brother!"

CHAPTER 23

RECONS LAST BATTLE/BROKEN ARROW

R eturning to the ship I kept thinking about what I had just gone through for the second time in the past two hours. My feet and legs, as they rested on the rudder pedals, began to shake involuntary, so I firmly placed them on the floor of the cockpit so that it was unnoticeable to my crew or co-pilot.

I began to doubt myself and wondered if I had reservations about returning to the cockpit. In all the missions I had flown up until this point never before had my body reacted as violently as this. My right hand began to tremble. I had to rid my mind of the dangers I just faced. I concentrated on returning to the ship.

There in the distance I saw the silhouettes of the ships. I centered in on the Princeton and made my way home. After landing I shut down the aircraft, crawled out of the cockpit and immediately was engulfed by a mass of humanity. They couldn't thank me enough for coming to their rescue. At that very moment all of them collectively would have given me all their worldly possessions. All I had to do was ask.

With all the thanks finally ended and everyone dispersing into the bowels of the ship I knew I still had work to do.

I quickly completed a post flight of the aircraft and found a number of problems. I placed several entries into the aircraft's flight log: "Fuel tank leaking due to numerous ground fire hits, hydraulic quantity gage indicates leak somewhere in system, reads almost empty, engine running very rough, electrical system has too many items to place on page. Airworthy status: will not fly again. Throw overboard."

I said under my breath, "Good. My flying this night is over."

Thinking my day had ended and my missions were complete I learned the battle continued on for 12 members of the 3rd Recon Battalion. They were holding out on Hill 551 on Escape Route 2 but running out of ammunition. Outnumbered and surrounded they called, "Broken Arrow, Broken Arrow, about to be overrun."

Everyone and his neighbor were summoned to give aide the best they could. Rat Pack was busy sorting out the numerous aircraft, assigning altitude and directing traffic in and out of the bombing and strafing runs. They were keeping the enemy at bay.

The Marines on hill 551 were desperate. They prayed there was someone with enough courage or backbone to come and rescue them from hell. They were going to die; they knew it. Each man felt it. There had to be a chopper pilot somewhere that would take a chance and get them off that hill.

Twelve Marines were firing their weapons, killing the enemy and praying at the same time. All of them were praying for a chopper pilot with the balls of a high diver to come and get them.

After writing up my aircraft I started making my way down the ladder of the ship to the Ready Room. The moment I opened the door from the passageway and walked into the room, Col. Holiday greeted me, if you can call it a greeting. "Come with me; we're going to get some Marines off Hill 551 and bring 'em home."

I looked at him, part of me wishing I hadn't just heard his words.

"They're surrounded and about to die on top of that shithole," he continued. "they're calling Hill 551 home for the moment. They're holding their own, waiting for you and me to come and rescue their asses. You and Lt. Goodell will take EM24. You'll fly as Aircraft Commander. Your crew is already aboard the a/c, the checklists are complete and you'll fly wing on me, EM1. Let's go."

I blew out my breath and followed him.

Climbing out after takeoff, Holiday and I contacted Red Cross our cruiser and CIC.

"Red Cross, Red Cross, this is Candy Bar do you read?"

"Read you loud and clear, Candy Bar. Have you on radar. Pick up a heading 240 degrees, climb to 6500. Destination 24 miles. You have six F4 available for a combat cap, eight A4s working the area to the west of your destination. Twelve Marines awaiting your arrival."

The night was just about over, the morning sun just starting to lighten the skies for us to get a good visual of the surrounding area and of the LZ. The hilltop terrain was mostly flat with a few tree stumps in the

area to the north. Tall grass surrounded the entire area giving the NVA plenty of places to hide while approaching the summit of Hill 551.

The LZ was just large enough to hold one aircraft at a time. We were going to be second to pick up the final six men, which meant we're going to get the shit shot out of us during the pickup.

I could see the tracers as they made their way toward the LZ and CC. How many NVA were in the area was undetermined. All I knew was that there was a shit pot full of them shooting up the hilltop and CC's aircraft. Tracers everywhere. I passed the word to the Crew Chief and Straphanger that we were going to definitely be in harm's way. "Say a prayer. We have to have one answered this morning."

Col. Holiday called inbound. I watched and could see that he was under heavy fire. What seemed like five minutes, but was really only seconds, I was already inbound when the Colonel called, "Coming out. Six Marines still holding their own."

At about 150 feet the NVA had us in their sights. We were taking so many hits they were too numerous to count. Round after round struck the aircraft just about everywhere. Several A4 aircraft made extremely low passes suppressing some if not all of enemy fire for the moment.

My landing wasn't the best, but I didn't give a shit. Over the intercom I told the Crew chief to get the men onboard quickly so we could get out of here. In the meantime the Straphanger kept firing his weapon on the area to our left. All the while, the Crew Chief screamed, "We got 'em all, Captain. Let's get out of here!"

The Marines we were extracting began to fire their weapons out the window openings of the aircraft, adding suppressing fire into the NVA-occupied area.

I didn't need to hear the Crew Chief tell me to get outta there twice.

Pulling up on the collective, I departed the LZ without hesitation. At about 50 feet LT. Goodell was hit in the face. The shot almost tore his helmet off. Falling forward, the weight of his body landed against the cyclic, which forced the nose of the a/c into a diving position. I thought we were going in.

Reaching over with my free hand, I pulled him back toward his headrest and quickly locked his shoulder harness. I gently pulled back on the cyclic as we sped down the eastern slope of Hill 551. I have never, unintentionally or otherwise, been this close to the ground about to crash and escaped tragedy with my heart racing at 120 beats/per. Looking over at Goodell it was obvious he was dead.

Seconds later I was hit in the hip and then again in the left shoulder. I still had control of the a/c and continued my climb to altitude out of the range of small arms fire. I called for an escort. With that the Colonel turned around and joined up on my wing.

Calling me on the radio, the Col. Asked, "How you doing, Big Guy?"

I replied, "To be perfectly honest, Sir, there is so much blood in this cockpit that I don't know if it's the co-pilot's or mine. I'm soaked from shoulder to hip and I'm cold. Chilled to the bone. Do we have far to go, Colonel? I don't have a visual on the ship. Help me, Colonel;

I've got a crew of three and six Marines counting on me to bring 'em home. Struggling. I'm starting… My vision… Things… blurry."

"Look, Ryan, you got four miles to go and one more landing to make before you begin thinking about FLYING WEST. You can make it. Keep your head up. Do you see the ship?"

"I do. Call Flight Ops… Tell them I'm inbound. Crew of three and six passengers for a final."

CHAPTER 24

CASUALITIES AND INJURED PARTIES

Back in my office, I watched the expression on my grandson's face. It said everything. He was in awe of his father… my son, Jason Ryan.

I took up where my son's voice had stopped in the story.

"Your father made his last successful carrier landing at 0632 hours on the U.S.S. Princeton somewhere in the South China Sea," I said softly. "His last successful act had been to cut the mixture to the engine, slowly engage the rotor brake and set his parking brake. With his final checklist completed he laid his head back on the headrest, closed his eyes, took one more deep breath and, with mission complete, he was gone. A hero."

I reached out to place my hand on Kirk's shoulder. "A hero," I repeated.

"With Operation At Morning's Light ending and Task Force 34.21 making its way back to Okinawa, Japan, Colonel Holiday called for and requested a meeting of all able bodied men to muster on the hanger deck at 1300 hours the following day. He needed to speak to the survivors of the 3rd Recon Battalion and the men of Joshua. He

wished he could speak to the aircraft flying CAP at that time, but it just wasn't possible. Back at Naha that would take place.

"At precisely 1300 hours the Colonel began by saying he was proud to have served in such a distinguished Marine outfit."

He said, "A Marine takes his oath to serve his country and does it of free will. He accepts the fact that he may be called upon to do the impossible. This past night our Corps called us to the steps of despair. We were asked to possibly surrender our lives for our fellow man. The following men have done just that. These gallant Marines have given their lives to set men free."

He then slowly read the names:

Capt. Jason E. Ryan, USMC
Capt. Michael J. Scali, USMC
Capt. Tyler D. Smith, USMC
Capt. Robert G. Barnes, USMC
1st Lt. George A. Goodell, USMCR
Staff Sgt. Raymond C. Woodruff, USMC
Lance Cpl. Bruce R. Hatfield, USMC

Members of the 3rd Recon Battalion KIA:

Capt. Phillip R. Scanlon, USMC
PFC Clyde A. Waters, USMC
PFC Donald S. Clemente, USMC
PFC Charles G. Robin, USMC
Cpl. Marty R. Long, USMCR

Cpl. Steven R. Spain, USMCR
Cpl. Jose A. Medina, USMCR
Sgt. William G. Acosta, USMCR
Sgt. David S. Christopher, USMCR

The officer continued. "This Command lost seven brave Marines and have 12 WIAs, four of whom are in serious condition. It is with great pain and unlimited sorrow that I post their names on the bulletin boards in the pilot ready room for all hands to view.

"Going into this operation we knew the success rate would be approximated 90% give or take 5%. We have given up 16 Marines – pilot, crew and recon – to save the following:

Two Air Force F4 Weapons Systems Officers
Two Navy Pilots
Three Marine Pilots
Ten Air Force pilots
Four U. S. Marine Infantry
Four Vietnamese Officers
Three Coast Guardsmen

"Totals 24 U. S. Personnel/4 Vietnamese Personnel. Grand total 28 Servicemen extracted from Jericho.

"Sixteen KIAs: seven from our unit, nine from the 3rd Recon Battalion in exchange for twenty-eight POWs. We knew the odds of pulling this off without losing some personnel would be extremely high and that it would be costly in human life. To those we have saved our mission has been a success. To our brothers who have lost their lives their

mission has not been a failure but a sacrifice. They have given all they have to set their fellow man free."

The Colonel continued steadfastly, barely taking a breath. "Those that perished came from all walks of life. They came from tiny villages, small towns, and large cities… from all points of the compass. Someone's father, someone's husband, son, uncle, cousin or brother is now going home to be placed in his final resting place.

"If you have lost a roommate please go back to your quarters and go through their gear to list, verify and pack all noteworthy items. Have all uniforms and personal clothing cleaned, packaged and placed into his footlocker so it can be returned with the remains. Please use good judgment and destroy all sensitive items that might be an embarrassment for the family. After completion of this task visit your brothers in sickbay. They need to know you're still there for them.

"It pains me to say that your mission and what you have done will be hidden from history for several years. All After Action Reports will be classified Top Secret and designated NOT TO BE OPENED UNTIL AUTHORIZED BY THE HIGHEST OF AUTHORITY. That is by direct order of the President of the United States.

"The Marine Corps has approved the Silver Star to all personnel participating in Operation At Morning's Light except one. Captain Jason E. Ryan will receive not only the Silver Star but also the Navy Cross for participation in two missions while attached to this unit.

"There will not be any official ceremony in receipt of this award. Your record book will not reflect any date of receipt for this commendation

and the authorizing of this medal will be approved and classified Top Secret by the Commandant of the U. S. Marine Corps. Your SRB will reflect you have the medal by authorization of the Commandant of the Marine Corps only. On your uniform you may wear this ribbon with pride.

"There will not be any citations written or dispersed to any individual for this medal. One for each of you will be at Headquarters Marine Corps under classified documents. Hopefully someday these documents will be declassified and the world will know what you have done for your country and your fellow man. Admin personnel will be cutting new orders for you and forwarding them to you prior to our arrival in Naha. Any Questions?"

I finished this part of the story by telling Kirk, "With none to be asked, the CO told everyone they were dismissed."

CHAPTER 25

LAST LETTERS HOME
A STRANGER AT MY DOOR

I told Kirk that among the personal items found in his father's room were two letters. One was addressed to his wife Martha and sealed in its envelope. The other was to his son, but was incomplete still sitting on his desk. The person surveying the room saw to it that both letters would be forwarded to the proper parties.

I ended the story by saying, "The demands placed on your father's shoulders that last day of his life, and the things he was ordered to do for his country and his fellow man was unusually challenging and fulfilling his duty that day was above and beyond the call of duty."

"This entire story that I just passed to you was shared with me by Captain James McGray, USMC. One warm summer day a man knocked on my door, introduced himself and asked to come in so he could tell me about your father... my son. Your dad was this man's close friend. He told me the story I just told you and handed me two letters before leaving."

Reaching down to the right hand bottom drawer of my desk I withdrew two letters. Holding one up, I said, "This one is your mother's. She asked to share it with you; she received her letter long

ago."

Then I held up the other letter. "This one is for you," I explained. "It's time for you to read it. Afterward, I want you to read the letter that your father wrote to your mother. It will tell you how much he loved her."

Kirk read quietly, not looking up until he was finished with the first letter. It read:

******

February 12, 1976
Somewhere in the pacific

Dear Kirk,

I have a little time to write a few lines to you and will probably have to finish this letter when I return from a journey I'm not anxious to start. What will be will be.

I know I'm missing a lot of your prime time on the gridiron and every game you play while I am away is time forever lost. I totally enjoy the write-ups in the newspapers your mom encloses in her letters. The articles certainly keep me up to date, not only of your team but your stats. You are some football player!

I know scholarships are coming as your mom tells me she has received a number of letters as well as phone calls from coaches throughout the country. Keep up the good work. I'm proud of

what you're doing on the field but even happier about your classroom accomplishments. A 3.85 GPA should get you into any college that offers you a scholarship in football or baseball.

I'm sorry I'm away from home so much, son, and I know you're hurt when the Corps calls me away to do my duty for my country. You must know by now and recognize that my life would be incomplete were it not for my being an officer and pilot in the Corps. I truly love my work and my country.

Our goals are different. You are an academic and an athlete and it shows in everything you have done these many years. It has been wonderful to watch you grow and develop as a young man in sports and in school. You have two avenues to go forward on, sports or your choice in academic studies.

You are such a bright young man who within the next few years will be making decisions that will affect you the rest of your life. Whatever avenue you choose you must remember there is a consequence that will be either virtuous or troublesome. Choose your path wisely. Keep your head held high and feverishly work toward your goals.

I made a covenant with myself a long time ago. I would always take to task any undertaking with a supreme effort and blame only myself if I should fail. Give nothing less than a Champion's effort in all that you choose to do and you will not fail.
I'm in pain for you as you struggle to make the decisions you have on your table. You must choose between college, football, or baseball. Remember for every action there is a reaction. The ball is

in your court as they say, so choose wisely.

Say a few prayers, and talk to your mom, your coach and academic counselor. Gather up all your information and let God guide you where you need to go. He will always be there for you.

The life I have chosen for myself has made me very happy. You must do the same. Walk your own path and…

****

The letter ended there. Kirk looked up at me.

After reading the letter from his father to him, Kirk wondered how it might have ended. He then slowly opened the letter to his mother and began to read the private thoughts of a husband to his wife.

****

February 12, 1976

My Dearest Martha,

At this very moment I am aboard the U.S.S Valley Forge somewhere on the South China Sea. The night is dark, the sea is calm and our ship is just one of many in a task force headed for somewhere off the coast of this country that I am not allowed to disclose. I'm not keeping any secrets from you any longer.

I've never visited this area before. However, a U. S. Marine Corps

General has handpicked this compound where a multitude of bad guys live and are holding U.S. Prisoners and men of our U.S. Forces. They are men who want to return to their homeland and we're going to help them with their journey home.

Before I set out on this mission I am writing to you to tell you just what you have meant to me the many years we have been together. You are the only woman in my life and I am full of pride when I say I love you so very much. You are my life's gift, my beautiful standalone trophy.

I remember the first time we met. I believe it was the Exchange at El Toro. You were looking at jewelry and as I passed you, you were looking at some rings at the counter. I told you I would buy that for you if you'd marry me today. I was serious and you looked at me as if I was a crazy fool wandering around loose that perhaps should be arrested and placed in a loony bin. Needless to say, you found the humor in me and finally accepted my invitation to dinner that evening. We were married seven days later. I assume you grew tired of my begging.

It has been a wonderful marriage filled with excitement, disappointment, packing and unpacking, but mostly it's been years of a loving relationship that brought to us a wonderful son. I wouldn't change a thing.

I love you with all my heart. See you when this is all over. Must write Kirk now.

You loving husband,
Jason

******

With that Kirk asked me if I would leave him alone for a few minutes
so he could digest what he had just heard and read.

Without delay I rose from my chair and left the room, but not before
I heard my grandson speak. I probably shouldn't have, but I listened
just outside the door.

As if his father were listening from Heaven, Kirk got up from his
chair, walked over to the window and looked skyward. "I miss you
dad and wish you were here to help me with the many decisions I
have to make in the very near future," he said. "If ever I needed you,
it's now. I'm trying to remember the many pathways you brought to
light as I grew to adulthood. You've taught me well.

"Right now I'm looking back to when I was a small boy and you
coached me in Little League. What a great team we had! As I search
my memory I remember you forcing me to play catcher. I hated it yet
I adjusted to the position and started to get better and better. Now
that I've grown older and have all those youthful seasons behind the
plate, I'm one of the best catchers in the country. I'm constantly being
pursued by various baseball teams; mostly the Philadelphia Phillies.
"I remember that wherever your duty stations might take us and I
played football you would go to all my practices. You never missed
any of them if you were home and not deployed. From Pop Warner

182

to my freshmen year you were always standing on the sideline encouraging me to pursue the runner and to hit harder and harder.

"I hurt you when I asked you not to come to my practices any longer. I never read the pain in your eyes but your heart later told the whole story. Mom told me you went up on a hill in the surrounding area and watched my practices through binoculars. While doing so someone must have called the police as a patrol car came by and you had to explain yourself. After a simple explanation the two of you watched number 44 practice for about ten minutes and then the police officer made you move along by request.

"Our fireside talks as we sat by the fire pit are what I miss the most. It was open season on any subject talking about anything that came to mind, politics, sports, religion, school, homework and, of course, girls. Just sitting there with you with the flames keeping us warm, being together and quietly listening to the occasional crackling sound of the wood burning made our day complete.

"I remember you always kept an eye on that watch of yours. You were never late for anything. At 9:00 p.m. sharp we were required to go inside and watch the evening news. You always said it was important to keep up with the subject matter of what was happening in the world and in our local community.

"What is missing from my life the most is the friendship that you and I shared as far back as I can remember. You were not only my father guiding me in the world, feeding and clothing me but you were a close friend. We were pals, buddies.

"I have tried to mold myself into a replica of you and everything you stand for. You were my role model and mentor as I grew to be a man. All the things you have passed along to me I will pass along to my son when I have one. You were a wonderful man and any young man would treasure you as their father but you were mine.

"You loved the Corps and you sacrificed your life for your fellow man. You truly loved my mother and I pray I become the man that you were in serving God, Country, Corps and family."

I could hear that my grandson was crying softly as he spoke the final words to his father.

"Dad, Rest In Peace and God Bless You."

GLOSSARY

AUTO ROTATION	TO GLIDE IN SUCCESSFULLY
A/C	AIRCRAFT
AWOL	ABSENT WITHOUT LEAVE
BOQ	BACHELORS OFFICERS QUARTERS, BILLETED ASSIGNMENTS
BACK PACK	GROUND UNITS
CAP	COMBAT AIR PATROL
CIC	COMBAT INFORMATION CENTER
CO	COMMANDING OFFICER
COL.	COLONEL
DMZ	DEMILITARIZED ZONE
EXEC/XO	SECOND IN COMMAND OF A UNIT
EVAC	EVACUATION
FIELD DAYING	CLEANING UP
HQ	HEADQUARTERS
HP	HORSE POWER
H AFTER TIME	MEANS "HOUR"
HEAD	TOILET
0630Hrs	TIME (HOURS)
KIA	KILLED IN ACTION
LZ	LANDING ZONE
LT.	LIEUTENANT

LPH	LANDING PLATFORM HELICOPTER
MIA	MISSING IN ACTION
MP	MILITARY POLICE
MARTD	MAR AIR TRAINING DETACHMENT
MAINSIDE	MAIN MILITARY BASE IN AREA
MESS HALL	DINING ROOM
NVA	NORTH VIETNAM ARMY
NAS	NAVAL AIR STATION
OP	OUTPOST
POW	PRISIONER OF WAR
RAT TRAP	CALL SIGN
RECON	RECONNAISSANCE
RPG	ROCKET PROPELLED GRANADE
REQUALS	REQUALIFACATIONS
STRAIGHT AWAY	RIGHT THEN, IMMEDIATELY
SEMPER FI	ALWAYS FAITHFUL
STRAPHANGER	GUNNER AT WINDOW
T/O	TAKE OFF
IN TRAIL	ONE BEHIND THE OTHER
SRB	SERVICE RECORD BOOK

MILITARY RANKS

PVT.	PRIVATE
SGT.	SERGEANT
GYSGT.	GUNNERY SGT. GUNNY
MSGT.	MASTER SGT.
2ND LT.	SECOND LIEUTENANT
1ST LT.	FIRST LIEUTENANT
CAPT.	CAPTAIN
MAJ.	MAJOR

LT COL.   LIEUTENANT COLONEL
GEN.   GENERAL

VIETNAM WAR STATISTICS

MYTH: The Vietnam War has had millions of articles, countless books, cinemas and documentaries thrown out to the public erroneously portraying the American Serviceman as an evil representative of the United States. THIS IS FALSE!!

91% of those that fought were brave and honorable men who were proud to have served. 74 % said they would serve again.

North Vietnam made attacks on civilians the foundation of their strategy and the NVA soldiers that did so received commendations.

Americans that deliberately killed innocent people or were involved in some way received prison sentences and dishonorable discharges from their respective services.

97% of our veterans were discharged honorably – only ½ of 1 % have been arrested and incarcerated for crimes.

85% went on with their lives after the war and their personal income has exceeded non Vietnam Veterans by 18%.

MYTH: Most Vietnam Veterans were drafted. THIS IS FALSE!!

Two thirds of these vets were volunteers, and 70% of those killed were volunteers. Charles Moskos and John Sibley Butler in their recently

published book, All That We Can Be, reported that 86% of the men were Caucasians, 12.5% were African American, and 1.2% were other races. As of November 1993, of the men in the national database 58,148 are listed as KIA.

Deaths	Number	Average age
Total	58,148	23.11 years
Enlisted	50,274	22.37 years
Officer	6,598	28.43 years
Warrants	1,276	24.73 years
E1	525	20.34 years
USMC	14,844	20.46 years
11B ARMY	18,465	22.55 years

One 16-year-old was killed in Vietnam, Paul J Raber.

Oldest man killed was 62 years of age, Kenna Clyde Taylor.

11,465 KIAs were less than 20 years of age.

Approximately 11,000 military women were stationed in Vietnam. They were nurses, physicians, intelligence officers, and air traffic controllers, Red Cross Volunteers, USO and the Catholic Relief Services.

One out of every ten who served in Vietnam was a casualty.

58,148 KIAs, 304,000 WIA, 2.59 million served in the war.

At this date 2,200 are still MIA. 55 incidents of American servicemen

who were last seen alive still aren't accounted for. 500 pilots lost in Laos never returned.

MEDEVAC helicopters flew nearly 500,000 missions, average time from being wounded to hospital less than one hour.

2.4 million tons of bombs were dropped on the Ho Chi Minh Trail, almost twice the amount U.S. Forces dropped on all of Germany during World War ll.

12,000 helicopters saw action in Vietnam.

63 journalists were killed in the war.

Statistics Gathered From the following sources:
1. Gen. Westmoreland
2. All That We Can Be, written by Charles Moskos and John Butler
3. Speech by Lt. Gen Barry McCaffrey, Assistant to the Joint Chiefs of Staff, Memorial Day 1993
4. CACF: Combat Area Combat File
5. Vietnam in HD Video

CPSIA information can be obtained
at www.ICGtesting.com
Printed in the USA
FSOW03n1647051117
40685FS